Informed Faith

Reasons For The Hope Within

With Discussion Questions

by
Winston T. Sutherland, Ph.D.

Available At:
https://www.createspace.com/5132216
http://www.amazon.com/dp/1533630860
http://www.amazon.ca/dp/1533630860
http://www.amazon.co.uk/dp/1533630860
http://www.amazon.de/dp/1533630860
http://www.amazon.es/dp/1533630860
http://www.amazon.fr/dp/1533630860
http://www.amazon.it/dp/1533630860

Contact Author At:
Sutherland.af@gmail.com

This book is dedicated to
Amy Sutherland who taught me,
*Dare not trust the sweetest frame
but wholly lean on Jesus name.*

CONTENTS

LIST OF ILLUSTRATIONS

ACKNOWLEDGEMENTS

Preparing the manuscript for publication would have been much more difficult without the helpful assistance of caring family and friends: Dr. Adrian Walcott, Pastor Rick Spenst, Pastor Romain Zannou, Dr. Ibiyinka Solarin, Dr. Dwight Fennell, Elder Moses Sutherland, Professor Germaine Albuquerque, Bro. Roger Daniel of Believer's Bookshelf, and my beloved wife Magna. Thank you all for your invaluable contributions.

PREFACE

What could be more important than faith? It is our doorway to God. As members of the human family each of us embarks on a journey the moment we are conscious of our existence. As soon as we know we exist, existential questions probe our minds. Who am I? Why am I here? What is this all about? These questions drive our search for meaning. They lead us on a quest culminating in a personal philosophy of life.

Of course, not everyone uses the label "Faith" to describe their belief system; some use very different labels to identify their way of life, and others, no labels at all. But regardless of the tag we use, whether we realize it or not, we all manage to form our own philosophy of life. We each develop our own belief system.

You would agree everyone's journey is different. Each search is as distinct as each person is unique. Mine, for instance, was influenced by my own inimitable personality, my family values, my religious upbringing, and my cultural background. And it began to take shape in my earliest days with questions like:

Who am I? Why am I here? What does all this mean?

I thought to myself,

I wake up in the morning, eat breakfast, play with my siblings, do my chores around the house, and go to sleep at night only to repeat the cycle the next day. What is this all about? What does this all mean?

As I gaze deep into the rearview mirror, I understand now that I was seeking to solve the mystery of the "God-human" relationship which has been shrouded by sin. The answers to those searching questions came later on in life through an encounter with the Almighty. I know somehow that God was drawing me to Himself. When I finally surrendered my life to Jesus Christ after years of resisting His persistent knocking on the door of my heart, all those questions were immediately answered. Suddenly my existence made sense. God filled me with unspeakable joy, incomprehensible peace and an unshakable assurance which can't be humanly explained. I was infused with new life, the life of God within me. My excitement and confidence in my joy-filled faith drove me to study the Bible relentlessly.

Unable to contain my happiness, I began to tell others about my encounter with God. Some were curious, others were receptive, but many were skeptical, even hostile to the message of God's amazing love for us. One particular experience stands out from times of sharing the good news.

My job was located in the middle of Times Square in New York City where millions of tourists flock to vacation each summer. During my lunch break I took a stack of gospel tracts and gave them out to the crowds teeming up and down the busy sidewalk. Most people politely accepted them and kept on walking while occasionally some would stop and I'd have a chance to chat with them.

One day a well-dressed man in his forties challenged me with questions examining the foundations of my faith. His questions tested the credibility of the Bible, the trustworthiness of miracles, and the claim that Jesus is the only way to God. Although I had considered those questions before, I must admit I found myself unable to provide satisfactory answers.

Now, I was fortunate to attend a church which upheld the Bible as the Word of God and where I enjoyed fellowship with like-minded believers. But the weight of those questions that day while attempting to persuade others to "Taste and see that the Lord is good," forced me to consider other important aspects of my faith. That unnamed traveler seemed to be saying to me,

> You are asking me to believe in Jesus Christ? You believe the Bible; how do you know the Bible is true? Who wrote it? How can we be certain the Bible is trustworthy? What about other religions? What makes this one the right one?

My impulse was to resist what I thought he was implying—that the Bible wasn't trustworthy, that men with all their imperfections and biases wrote the Bible, and that other religions were just as legitimate as Christianity. But I sensed God saying to me, "Those are legitimate, fair, and reasonable questions." Actually, the stranger echoed some of the questions I entertained privately at one time or another. If I am going to ask others to entrust their souls and their eternal destinies to Jesus Christ shouldn't I be able to provide answers to reasonable queries they have about believing in Him? Those questions also exposed my own personal need to investigate and know the truth.

I don't mind being wrong about many things in life; but, I cannot afford to be wrong about my soul's eternal destiny.

Now ultimate certainty comes from God Himself, from the assurance His Spirit gives to believers. Paul the apostle made that clear when he said,

The Spirit Himself bears witness with our spirit that we are sons of God.

—Romans 8:16

The good news is that we can be certain. God wants us to be certain, not merely wish and hope, but to know for certain. His spiritual salvation is, by nature, secure; it's full-proof.

Two strong charges have been given to believers in this matter, especially as we discern the nearness of the Lord's promised return. The first is from the apostle Peter who gave instruction that we should always be prepared to provide an answer to anyone who asks about the hope we have within. The second is from Jude who instructs us to earnestly contend for the faith which was delivered to the saints once for all (Jude 3). ["The faith" here refers to the body of teachings which was delivered to the church by first-century apostles of Christ.]

For this and other reasons, I enrolled at a theological seminary—an educational institution specializing in the Bible. Not that I had doubts about the integrity of my faith, (as mentioned earlier, God's Spirit testified to my spirit that I am His), but because it was sensible to investigate its foundation and to be better prepared to give an answer to any who asks about the hope I have within. Luke wrote to Theophilus,

> It seemed fitting for me as well, having investigated everything carefully from the beginning, to write it out for you in consecutive order, most excellent Theophilus; so that you might know the exact truth about the things you have been taught.
>
> —Luke 1:3-4

I was not disappointed. During my first semester, I explored questions of the Bible's credibility looking into its inspiration and canonicity. These were found to be in agreement with my experience with God and His Word, the Bible.

I also found that asking the hard questions about your faith may lead to one of two discoveries.

1. You might discover that your faith was founded upon shaky ground which is better to learn sooner rather than later.

2. You may confirm that your faith is built on the truth, which will lead to greater confidence.

My search led to greater confidence. My faith was strengthened and I enjoy a deep and abiding relationship with Jesus Christ. A belief system founded on truth has that effect.

I have since engaged in countless discussions on faith with individuals from different backgrounds. Some relegate faith to the marginal in society, such as the poor and needy, and the little old lady who needs a crutch to lean on. "No truly intelligent person," they say, "really believes in God!" "People of faith are desperate, uninformed, or misinformed" they argue. But in fact, they are the truly misinformed ones. Faith is not thin and weak. It is robust and strong. It is not only for those our world considers the lowly of society but for all people, rich and poor, noble and ignoble.

I have found Jesus' declaration to be the Son of God, true. After thorough investigation, the evidence is undeniable that the Bible is true. More and more I find myself agreeing with poet and author G. K. Chesterton:

The Christian ideal has not been tried and found wanting;
it has been found difficult and left untried.

Millions who share our planet receive their faith passed on to them as a tradition, usually from their parents. That's not bad in itself; but this is, most people never bother to investigate its claims. Some things in life are too important to accept without examination (Proverbs 16:25). And one's personal faith tops that list of critical things necessitating as much certainty as possible. Paul warns believers in Christ:

> See to it that no one takes you captive through philosophy and empty deception, according to the tradition of men, according to the elementary principles of the world, rather than according to Christ. For in Him all the fullness of Deity dwells in bodily form, and in Him you have been made complete, and He is the head over all rule and authority.
>
> —Colossians 2:8-10

I am thankful that a friendly stranger challenged me with hard questions about my faith. For a brief time it was uncomfortable thinking "what if" questions. But his challenge served to heighten my pursuit of an informed faith.

Winston T. Sutherland

AUTHOR'S NOTE

The New Testament calls upon believers in Christ to be vigilant about their faith. The apostle Peter says,

> Be ready always to give an answer to everyone who asks you for a reason of the hope that is in you.
>
> —1 Peter 3:15

It's only reasonable to know *why* we believe what we believe. As the reality of the end times draws near, the need to be sure your faith is anchored to the Rock, Jesus Christ, is made more critical.

Informed Faith discusses those reasonable questions deserving of thoughtful answers. In it, biblical faith takes the witness-stand ready to face interrogation from all. This brings us to you, the reader.

Who Should Read This Book?

Everyone!

Everyone's faith should be an informed faith, not a blind one. But some groups with particular interest include:

- ❖ College students exposed to various ideologies in the classroom and on campus;
- ❖ Church groups who desire to go deeper in Christ and explore important questions about their faith. *End of chapter questions are provided to facilitate group discussion;*
- ❖ Young-adult groups;
- ❖ Anyone training for the ministry should be ready to provide answers to the people they will serve;
- ❖ Individuals who desire to be always ready to provide an answer to anyone who asks about their hope—that what they pledge their lives to is worthy of them.

May this book be as much a blessing to you as it has to me writing it! Above all, may we glorify God with an informed faith.

Getting The Most Out Of This Book

Some books may be read quickly. This is not one of them. A contemplative, meditative read is recommended. Slow down and ponder; preferably, next to an open Bible so you can look up references. This subject requires a careful treatment, thoughtful consideration.

Be open. Ask God to lead you in this important quest. Being closed will serve to complicate the process.

Enjoy the journey of faith discovery, faith recovery, and faith intimacy.

Finally, spread the word; gossip the word.

SECTION I

INTRODUCING INFORMED FAITH

Chapter 1

Faith's Majesty

Faith enables persons to be persons,
Because it lets God be God.
—Carter Lindberg

Among God's many gifts to us, faith has proven essential for our existence. Like the air we breathe, no one can live without it. Yet, many never give faith a second thought. Often taken for granted, untold numbers are oblivious to the privileged position it occupies. But faith's importance isn't diminished because people fail to acknowledge it. Whether we think about breathing or not, oxygen is still critical for our survival.

Upon faith, God hangs His very glory, His splendor, His majesty. Without faith, we cannot see Him in His true light. Through faith some have commanded the sun to stand still in its tracks. By faith people have moved the hand of God to shut the mouths of ravenous lions. Others withstood unthinkable fears and basked in reassuring peace when circumstances dictated every fiber of their beings to scream panic and worry. Because of faith, believers have been emboldened to square-off against the otherwise frightening powers of darkness. By faith, God brings the human race into intimacy with Himself. People who live by faith experience exhilarating glory; they triumph over the cares and anxieties this world so often threatens. Yes, faith is among God's absolute finest gifts to humankind.

DEVALUATION OF FAITH

For all its majesty, faith is often misunderstood and dismissed as unimportant. Probably because it is intangible, many overlook its value. People of faith are commonly viewed as unlearned, unintelligent, and stuck in the dark ages. Somewhere along the way, it became unfashionable to be a person of faith.

But faith's proven track record exposes the absurdity of such flawed notions. Christians are to be found at the highest levels of most major fields and industries. Believers have occupied the highest offices in many nations scattered all across our planet. They have led teams in scientific research, and have been competitive with the brightest minds our world has produced.

In spite of this, people who practice faith have been repeatedly marginalized and cast in a bad light. Often the butt of Hollywood's jokes, Christians remain a staple on the menu of late-night comedians. Ironically, it is to people of faith that our world looks for answers, hope, and assistance in moments of crises the magnitude of Hurricane Katrinas and World Trade Center bombings. (Many churches reported a rise in attendance during the aftermath of the horrendous 9-11 terrorist attacks.) For all its supremacy, for many, faith is not a cherished commodity.

Millions of people exhibit an over-reliance upon their senses. They tend to depend exclusively upon tangible evidence, the kind their five senses approve, their sight, hearing, sense of smell, things they can handle, and taste. They boast, "If I can see it, I will believe it. If I can touch it, then I'll take it seriously. The more my natural senses are involved, the closer I will be to believing it." Jesus, over two thousand years ago, questioned this human tendency to devalue faith when He sighed,

> When the Son of Man comes, will He find faith on the earth?
>
> —Luke 18:8

What then has happened to this precious gift to humankind?

CENTRALITY OF FAITH

It's an age old practice to speculate about the nature of the forbidden fruit. But the kind of fruit had little to do with the purpose of its placement in the midst of Eden's paradise. Neither was the pivotal question merely a matter of Adam and Eve's will to devour the edible delight. Effectively, it was a question of faith. Inasmuch as God placed "The Tree of Knowledge of Good and Evil" in the center of Eden, it tested what was central to God—loyalty! Faith! In whom will our first parents believe? Who will they trust? Who will they obey? With whom will their loyalties lie? In whom will they have faith? Will they be persuaded by God or the serpent? That's the central issue!

Never had the human race been faced with a decision bearing greater consequences. The answers to those questions determined the course our world took; it established how we as humans relate to our creator.

21

Our future as a race hinged upon that crucial dilemma—our lives depended upon the outcome of their decision. Humanity's collective faith stood trial that eventful day. And although no grim-faced judge dressed in flowing black robe sat in intimidating judgment, the placement of our first parents' faith sent shock waves still felt in every corner of the world today.

To this day, that question still bangs on the doors of conscience; it still occupies center stage in God's kingdom. Who will we believe? In whom will we have faith? For we all believe in someone or something.

Some people believe in the God of the Bible. Others believe in some other god distinct from the God of the Bible. A pantheon of gods has won the loyalty of millions; whereas, others believe in no god at all. Some place their trust in themselves as the only god they'll acknowledge while material things and possessions occupy the hearts of many. Everyone, even those in the remotest corners of the earth, believes in someone or something.

Even atheists (people who don't believe in the existence of God) believe in someone or something.

Faith is crucial to both the existence and wellbeing of humankind. Although some try to devalue faith, it has not lost its majesty at all; it is alive and well. It is central to God's dealings with mankind.

NECESSITY OF FAITH

Before God would accommodate humans in His presence, He requires faith. Every step toward Him must be accompanied by faith. The writer of the biblical book, Hebrews, left no doubt about this when he declared:

> He who comes to God must believe that He is, and that
> He rewards those who diligently seek Him.
> —Hebrews 11:6

Faith is absolutely necessary for our dealings with God.
Eternal life is granted only when we believe in His Son. No
other avenue is acceptable with Him.

Not only does our eternal destiny depend on our faith in
God, but He has also subjected to our faith in Him the
quality of life we may enjoy here and now.

Israel's beloved King David helped us better understand
this when he said,

> Blessed is the man . . . who delights in the law of the Lord.
> —Psalm 1:1-2

In other words, blessed is the person who delights in God,
living a life of faith. This blessing upon those who delights in
God's Word is not limited to material increase; it includes
friendship with God, inner peace, the respect of others, a
conscience at rest, emotional stability, and a host of intangible
benefits. The prophet Isaiah captured this idea when he said,

> God will keep in perfect peace those whose mind is stayed
> upon Him because they trust in Him.
> —Isaiah 26:3

So faith in God is a requirement for our wellbeing both here
and hereafter.

Why then is faith important to God to such an extent that
without it He cannot be pleased? Even our approach to Him

must be accomplished through the agency of faith. As we've seen, faith is prerequisite to having access to Him. With so much depending upon faith, why is it that much misunderstood? How can multitudes of people carelessly dismiss the notion of faith's importance?

An adventurous exploration into the realm of faith promises to be time well spent. To find a wiser investment of time poses a difficult challenge.

CHAPTER 1 DISCUSSION QUESTIONS

1. In what ways is faith majestic? Central?

2. What are some common ways faith is devalued in society?

3. How is faith related to *The Tree of Knowledge of Good and Evil*?

4. In what way is faith necessary for both here and the hereafter?

Chapter 2

What Is Faith?

True faith rests upon the character of God and asks no further proof
than the moral perfections of the One who cannot lie.
—A.W. Tozer

What are we talking about here? What is this faith? Had it been possible to slice off a sample of faith and observe it under a microscope, what would we find? Would we find signs of life? Would we find an energy source? What helpful understanding might we get? What is the fabric of faith?

Although faith isn't a tangible object from which a sample may be viewed under the powerful lenses of a microscope, it is possible to be examined in the laboratory of life. And it has. Through the ages, people have tried to capture its various nuances. Some missed the mark altogether producing myths; but others proved helpful capturing faith's essence.

MYTHS ABOUT FAITH

Sometimes when attempting to grasp intangible concepts such as faith, it proves helpful to clear up misconceptions associated with the concept in question. So it might be useful to first clarify what faith is not. And down through the ages many have misunderstood and misrepresented the nature of faith.

A common myth says that faith is guesswork. While faith may sometimes involve making future projections, to say it is guesswork reduces it to an approach which leaves no room for sensible reasoning.

Faith is not uncertain wonderings such as, "Oh, I hope things work out this time, but if not oh well," with a heavy sigh at the end of such sentiments.

It is not as Nietzsche the 19th century German philosopher said, "Not wanting to know what is true."

Neither is it as Thomas Henry Huxley, the self-proclaimed agnostic thought, "Often extremely irrational attempts to justify our instincts."

Faith is certainly not, "An illogical belief in the occurrence of the impossible" as was believed by Henry Louis Mencken, a journalist probably best remembered for his reporting of the infamous Scopes trial. This landmark legal case, you may remember, debated whether schools may teach the Bible's creation account or the theory of evolution.

Surely faith is not reserved for the poor little souls who can't do any better, who need a crutch to lean on.

Faith doesn't leave believers with feelings of uncertainty, skepticism, cynicism, despair, or doubt. In fact, it is not a feeling at all; it is a knowing. It doesn't require that we put aside reason and logic to rely solely upon sentiment, traditions, and emotions. It's not guesswork; it's not mindless, elusive hope. It is not thin, weak, wishing on a long-shot chance. No, none of these things describe faith.

TOWARD AN UNDERSTANDING OF FAITH

On the contrary, faith is companion to certainty. It is at home in the realm of confidence. It's a deep knowing within. Men and women who live by faith have a confident swagger; although, not an arrogant posture. They're self-assured, better yet, God-assured because of their faith. The dictionary informs us that,

> Faith involves belief-in, trust, obedience, loyalty, being persuaded, and confidence.

These are all parts of faith's nature. They are shades of meaning which combine to approach a rich understanding of faith.

John Calvin, the French theologian wrote, "Faith consists, not in ignorance, but in knowledge, and that, not only of God but also of the divine will."

Renowned poet and philosopher, Ralph Waldo Emerson was on to something when he declared, "All I have seen teaches me to trust the Creator for all I have not seen." Well said! This is the essence of informed faith. We'll define it later on in the chapter.

Someone once likened faith to, "The bird that feels the light and sings to greet the dawn while it is still dark."

The common thread passing through each of these statements is that they all expressed confidence in "the not yet known" because they were anchored to something in "the known." In each case faith was based on some measure of experience (Romans 1:20).

It is worth noticing that none were mindless or emotional groping around in the dark; none were desperate grasping at straws. These attempts at describing faith did not reference lack of logic, or lack of rationale. For, although faith transcends both logic and reason, they are important aspects of faith.

In the Bible, much of faith is directed to God. He is the object of our faith. He expects us to *believe* Him, *obey* Him, *trust* Him, be *loyal* to Him, be *persuaded* of Him, and have *confidence* in Him—all of which the dictionary describes.

It is the author of the biblical book Hebrews, however, who offers what many regard as the Bible's formal definition of faith. In the opening lines of the eleventh chapter we read,

> Faith is the substance of things hoped for; the evidence of things not seen.
> —Hebrews 11:1

So, biblical faith may be described as belief, trust, or confidence in God about things unseen. Faith renders people so persuaded of the unseen, that the writer of Hebrews recognizes it as *substance* and *evidence* or *tangible proof*.

But faith as a living, dynamic reality is better understood in the realm of experience, not through strict definitions. Its power is experienced when we go beyond ourselves and trust; it does not come from merely talking, discussing, or dissecting. It is learned through living moment by moment with God. It is refined in the crucible of life.

Moving beyond definitions, we get a better grasp of this living, dynamic faith when we observe it at work in a man's journey with God.

ABRAHAM'S JOURNEY OF FAITH

Abraham's Faith Tested

Every once in a while we find ourselves in situations which stretch us beyond ourselves; and, what God asks of Abraham certainly knocks the wind out of you. What God asked was so difficult, so counter intuitive, that it goes against every cell in your body. In Genesis 22 we read the gut-wrenching words:

> Now it came about after these things, that God tested Abraham, and said to him, "Abraham!"
> And he said, "Here I am."
> And he said, "Take now your son, your only son, whom you love, Isaac, and go to the land of Moriah; and offer him there as a burnt offering on one of the mountains of which I will tell you."
>
> —Genesis 22:1-2

Just reading those words makes my inwards weak. What a dilemma! What a hard thing for God to ask! I mean, ask him to give lots of money, or half of his estate, but not his only son Isaac, whom he adores. Isaac was the miracle son of his old age, the beloved son whom God Himself promised, and the son for whom he waited many years to receive.

In obedience, Abraham finds himself atop mount Moriah—the place of sacrifice. But what is he thinking? Is he really about to do this? That he was able to get past the quiet storm brewing in his mind and the churning of his stomach leads us to look into his recent journey with God. That tense moment causes our minds to wonder, 'How did he get here?' How did he get to a place where he would be willing to obey God in sacrificing his heir, his son? Each step toward that altar had to be motivated by something greater than his love for his son. Let's start at the beginning.

Abraham's Call

On a sunny Mesopotamian morning an unfamiliar voice pierced through the chatter of market-place voices crying out to their pagan idols. It was the unique voice of God, the peaceful, firm, tender, reassuring voice of the sovereign Lord. A voice Abraham never heard before. Stephen tells us, "The God of Glory appeared to Abraham" (Acts 7:2). The glorious God singled him out and called him away from serving other gods (Joshua 24:2). Here is the historical record,

> The Lord said to Abram,
> Go forth from your country,
> And from your relatives
> And from your father's house,
> To the land which I will show you;
> And I will make you a great nation,
> And I will bless you, and make your name great;
> And so you shall be a blessing;
> And I will bless those who bless you,
> And the one who curses you I will curse.
> And in you all the families of the earth shall be blessed.
> —Genesis 12:1-3

This was Abraham's initial call from God.

Prior to this, we find his name in a genealogical list linking his ancestry to Shem, one of Noah's three sons. It was sometime after the devastating flood which wiped out all living beings on the earth that this call came to him. When Noah and his family began to repopulate the earth, the clan from which Abraham descended settled in Ur of the

Chaldeans (Genesis 15:7; Acts7:2) where they worshiped pagan idols and tribal deities. Now the Chaldeans were wicked; they would be notorious for oppressing the people of God. But God called Abraham away from idol worship to know Him and to make Him known. He was to exchange the familiar for the unknown. And it is through his obedience in following God that we see the development of faith in him.

Abraham's Experiences with God

The next word we read in Genesis 12 tells us how Abraham responded. "So." Not "But" or "However." "So." God calls, *so* Abram went forth as the Lord had spoken to him. He obeys. When you hear the voice of God calling you, the only appropriate response is obedience.

Abraham is soon to find out however, that obediently following God is not without its challenges. Although he doesn't know it he's about to embark on a journey that will give him intimate knowledge of God's character. So Abraham takes his wife, his father, and his nephew, along with his possessions to the land of Canaan. Before you know it, Canaan is under severe famine. And although famines provide opportunity to prove a man's character, Abraham finds himself in God's school proving God's character.

1. First Challenging Experience—Famine & Fear

The famine forces Abraham towards Egypt. On his way to Pharaoh's land, one of his fears rears its ugly head pressuring him to put his wife in a compromising position.

Sweetheart, you won "Miss Ur of the Chaldeans." When the Egyptians see you they'll kill me and save you alive because of your beauty. So, when we get there, tell them you're my sister.

(She was his half-sister—daughter of his father, but not of his mother, Genesis 20:12.) Abraham's worst fears came true. Pharaoh took one look at Sarah and made her part of his harem. But God, who got them out of Ur, gets them out of Egypt. We read that,

> The Lord struck Pharaoh and his house with great plagues because of Sarai, Abram's wife . . . And Pharaoh commanded his men . . . they escorted him away, with his wife and all that belong to him.
>
> —Genesis 12:17-20

Those plagues had the desired effect. Pharaoh quickly gave back Abraham his wife and sent them on their way with all their belongings. Thankful that his life was spared, Abraham learned a valuable lesson: *God is loyal.* If God calls you, He will take care of you. He learned that he could count on God to provide for him during famines and to protect him from his worst fears.

2. Second Challenging Experience—War & Worry

Another experience whereby Abraham gained insight into the character of God came during the war of the kings. Genesis 14 describes an international war involving nine kings—four allied against a confederation of five. Because of where his nephew, Lot, settled in the plains of Sodom and Gomorrah; he and his family, were captured when the four allied kings plundered those cities. And when Abraham heard about this, he assembled a small army of his own and pursued the coalition forces to free his nephew. He defeated the kings and rescued his nephew, Lot.

Abraham took great risks in pursuing Lot. He could have lost his life and his possessions by getting involved in a war with allied kings. He also risked being a target for backlash. If he had any doubts before, Abraham now knows that he has God's full protection. With an army of home-trained men, he snatched his nephew from the clutches of a ruthless coalition, larger in number and more experienced in warfare.

But if Abraham thought that somehow by his own cunning he rescued Lot, God deployed His high-priest Melchizedek, who made it known that it is God who fights his battles; it was the Most High who delivered Lot:

> And he (Melchizedek) blessed him and said, "Blessed be Abram of God Most High, possessor of heaven and earth; and blessed be God Most High, *who has delivered your enemies into your hand.*
> —Genesis 14:19-20

3. Third Challenging Experience—Heirless & Old

Shortly after this, God spoke to Abraham again and assured him that He is his shield (protector) and that his reward (posterity) would be great. Abraham responded by asking, how would his reward be great since he was childless?

Childless. No man is happy to build an estate having enough servants to be trained for warfare yet fails to produce a son to inherit it. Abraham had it all, a beautiful wife and a thriving business. But he also had the scourge of manhood—no son to carry on his legacy. All his life the reward he desired most (a son, an heir) eluded him. In the hidden pain of his unspoken shame he had another opportunity to know the character of God intimately. So God took him to His divinity school.

He broke the wonderful news to him. Abraham was going to father a son. Now when God tells you that you are going to have a son, it's no small matter, it's no ordinary thing. God doesn't go around announcing to people that He is about to lift the embargo and give them children. Abraham, who is nearing 100 years with a wife approaching 90, finds himself a real challenge. On the one hand, he and his wife Sarah are too old; but, on the other, this is coming from God. So God took him outside to view the twinkling stars scattered across the vast sky and asked him to count them. If he was able to number them, so shall his descendants be. This son would heal the longing of his heart and keep his manhood intact; it would be the start of a special dynasty.

Baby Isaac finally arrived just as God promised. Abraham and Sarah are overjoyed. They never thought they would see this day. Abraham has seen enough. His joy is complete. God has proven Himself faithful to His Word, again. He knows now that nothing is too hard for God. He knows this the same way David knew it when he defeated the giant Goliath. He knew it the same way every child knows which parent to go to in times of need. He knew it from experience with God.

He saw God provide for him and his family during a severe famine. He felt Him calm his worst fears by fighting for him against Pharaoh. He knew God returned his nephew, Lot, from a ruthless coalition of allied forces, and now He crowns His loyalty to him by giving him a son to carry on his name when it was humanly impossible. Abraham is overjoyed about God. He knows God can be trusted.

Abraham's Faith Proven

Just when Abraham thought all his challenges in the school of God were over, God still had the biggest test for him. Now, God is asking him to offer up that son in sacrifice to Him. Let's revisit those gut-wrenching words:

> Now it came about after these things, that God tested Abraham, and said to him, "Abraham!"
> And he said, "Here I am."
> And he said, "Take now your son, your only son, whom you love, Isaac, and go to the land of Moriah; and offer him there as a burnt offering on one of the mountains of which I will tell you."
> —Genesis 22:1-2

What!? Am I hearing You right, Lord? It doesn't add up; it doesn't make sense. How could God be asking me to offer up my beloved heir whom He gave me in my old age? What about the promised descendants as plenteous as the stars above? And how am I going to explain this to Sarah? Abraham's response? Again the next word we read is, "so."

> *So* Abraham rose early in the morning and saddled his donkey, and took two of his young men with him and Isaac his son; and he split wood for the burnt offering, and arose and went to the place of which God had told him.
> —Genesis 22:3

We've come to expect Abraham to obey and he does. The question that's shouting inside me is, *What would move a man to offer up his beloved son to God simply because He said to do so?* No argument. No fight. From what we have seen in Abraham, the answer is *Faith in God's proven character.* His journey with

God provided him intimate insight whereby he came to know the character of God. He discovered God's loyalty and integrity. He came to know His ways. So when it came to the really hard thing, he was persuaded that God would be true to His Word. This is how the writer of Hebrews explains Abraham's courage.

> By faith Abraham, when he was tested, offered up Isaac; and he who had received the promises was offering up his only begotten son; it was he to whom it was said, 'In Isaac your descendants shall be called.' *He considered that God is able to raise him from the dead.*
>
> —Hebrews 11:17-19

Absolutely amazing! Abraham knew God would keep His word to multiply his descendants even if He had to raise Isaac from the dead. Only an experienced heart can have that type of faith. Only proven character has the right to ask for that kind of trust. The rest of the story is well known. Abraham was about to carry out his toughest assignment from God. But the moment he raised his knife to plunge into his son's heart, a voice called from heaven stopping him from harming the boy. No doubt Abraham recognized that voice at once. It said,

> Do not stretch out your hand against the lad, and do nothing to harm him; for now I know that you fear God since you have not withheld your son, your only son, from Me.
>
> —Genesis 22:12

I imagine his body collapsed into his son, the knife fell to the ground, and rivers of pent-up emotions streamed from his eyes. After the floodgates finally closed, he could see that a ram was caught in the thicket by its horns. It would be his son's replacement to offer to God as a burnt offering.

Abraham's faith in God's proven character was so secure he was willing to obey Him even if it meant giving up his son. He was confident in God because of their history through famine, worry, war, and in giving him a son in his old age. So when it came to the difficult thing of sacrificing his son, he had excellent reasons to trust Him.

Abraham's faith demonstrated what was described both in the dictionary and in Scripture. He believed in *God*, trusted *Him*, had confidence in *Him*, was obedient to *Him*, was loyal to *Him*, and he was persuaded by *Him*. It is clear he had faith. What's more, he had an informed faith.

INFORMED FAITH

This begs the question, what is informed faith? We know what faith is; but, what sets *informed* faith apart? Since faith is belief in something, since it is trust, obedience, loyalty, and confidence, what is *informed* faith? We get our answer from God's Word the Bible; it is replete with examples of informed faith. Let us look at three portions of Scripture together which capture the essence of informed faith.

The first is Eliphaz's words. When speaking to Job, the man whose faith God severely tested, Eliphaz explained:

> Look, we have investigated this, and it is true. Hear it, and apply it for your own good.
>
> —Job 5:27

That's the idea. Investigate and examine your faith for truth. Test it. Prove it. Know what it is. Be informed of its tenets.

The second is found in Luke 1:3-4. Luke wrote to Theophilus:

> It seemed fitting for me as well, having investigated everything carefully from the beginning, to write it out for you in consecutive order, most excellent Theophilus; so that you might know the exact truth about the things you have been taught.
>
> —Luke 1:3-4

Here again we see people investigating the things they have been taught in pursuit of the truth (Luke 1:3-4).

The third is also from Luke who wrote the book of Acts. In it, the first century Bereans of Greece embody the ideals of informed faith. When the apostle Paul presented the gospel of Jesus Christ in Berea, we read that:

> . . . they received the Word with great eagerness, examining the Scriptures daily, to see whether these things were so.
>
> —Acts 17:11

The Bereans wanted to confirm the good news of the gospel which they heard so they examined the Scriptures for truth.

These three references along with the rest of Scripture lead us to our definition of informed faith. It is . . .

The belief a person develops from proving the truth about God through obedience and examination of His Word.

Informed believers don't mindlessly believe; they must be convinced. They must be persuaded that what they have found isn't fool's gold. They must know that what they believe is the truth. This brings a deep conviction within, a deep knowing.

Informed faith persuades the head, the heart, and the spirit—not only the heart! It is birthed from a deep conviction which joins an unexplainable sense of certainty (*heart and spirit*) with wholesome reason (*head*). This faith is biblically based as we have already seen. Both the old and new testaments instruct us to,

> Love the Lord with all your heart, mind, and soul.
> —Deuteronomy 6:5; Mark 12:30; Luke 10:27

I haven't met too many people who are surprised that faith engages the heart and soul (or spirit); but, it is the involvement of the mind that has suffered the greatest neglect. Contrary to popular thought, faith does not require that we overlook the use of the mind. We must think matters through. What we believe must make sense. Thought is a necessary part of the faith process. Believing involves thinking and reasoning.

Informed faith examines the credibility and integrity of the suitors asking us to entrust ourselves to them. Not every idea, philosophy, or religion which sounds good deserves our trust. Informed believers want to know if these are worthy suitors. The ancient sages understood this. One proverb says,

> The first to state his case seems right, until his opponent comes and cross-examines him.
> —Proverbs 18:17

Informed faith asks, "How do people arrive at their faith?" How did I come to believe what I believe? It answers the questions, Did I believe simply because the people I respect most (Parent, Teacher, Elder, Imam, Guru, Pastor) told me what to believe? Do I believe because everybody around me seems to believe the same thing? It puts a spotlight on the question, How did I arrive at my faith? Informed faith says, I believe what I believe because, having weighed the other options, it makes the most sense to believe what I have come to believe.

Abraham's journey with God exemplifies informed faith. Although his environment teemed with idolatry, he proved the truth about God over and over. His confidence in God deepened with each step they took together. He believed more and more as their journey progressed. After God proved Himself over and over to him, He then expected Abraham to be loyal—to have faith. So He tested him to expose where his true loyalties lie.

As a result, informed faith stands in sharp contrast to blind faith which faced little or no investigation at all. (Chapter 4 looks at informed faith vs. blind faith). Many, at great risk, adopt a blind faith out of convenience, popularity, or pressure from others. But matters of eternal consequences are too great to take lightly. And the deeper, abundant life is too precious to forfeit due to blind faith. The stakes are too high to employ a blind approach to believing.

CHAPTER 2 DISCUSSION QUESTIONS

1. What are some common myths about faith?

2. What are some important aspects of faith?

3. What factors contributed to Abraham's courageous faith to obey God by sacrificing his son?

4. What does the author mean by informed faith?

SECTION II

SOUND BASIS FOR FAITH

Chapter 3

Informed Faith And The Bible

Truthful lips will be established forever,
but a lying tongue is only for a moment.
　　　　　　　　　　　　　　　—Proverbs 12:19

QUESTIONING THE BIBLE'S CREDIBILITY

When it comes to the question of faith as a central part of God's dealings with us, an important place to start is the credibility of the Bible. The Bible contains the blueprint for our life with God and our fellow man. If humans came with a user's manual, the Bible would be it. But how do we know the Bible is trustworthy? How can we be expected to believe a book that has been written thousands of years ago? Is it not outdated? Didn't men write the Bible? And if men wrote the Bible, aren't humans flawed and imperfect? So, must the Bible not be flawed and imperfect too? What part does faith play in our acceptance of the Bible? How much faith must I have to believe the Bible? Does it have to make sense or must I believe it simply because people say it is the Word of God and because it has been around for a long time?

I have a friend and colleague who challenged the Bible's credibility when he asked these questions. He came to our college to teach for a year. A very intelligent man, we enjoyed numerous exchanges on various topics of conversation ranging from similarities and differences in European culture, American culture, and Trinidadian culture to soccer, politics, and religion.

One of my favorite and memorable chats with my visiting friend (whom I will refer to as Thomas) centered upon the question of the Bible's credibility. Thomas made it clear that although he was a Christian, he was not very religious. Since I don't think of myself as religious either—I also do not believe God likes religion, He prefers relationship—I was curious to understand what Thomas meant when he said he was not religious. So I asked him if he believed in the Bible. He assured me that he was a thinking man and considered himself a critical thinker. I was glad to hear that as I think it is important to weigh the evidence on all sides of an issue before coming to a conclusion. I too am a critical thinker. This whole topic of informed faith promotes critical thinking—using reason with faith, not just emotionally or blindly committing one's self in faith. But I didn't quite get an answer to my question. So I tried again to determine what he meant by his statement that he was not very religious. He thought for a while and then said that he believed in the four Gospels but he was unsure about the rest of the Bible especially the Old Testament. Upon hearing that, I thought about it for a while and then suggested to him that I was left puzzled. Fully aware that discussing matters of religion and personal belief had the potential to generate more heat than light, I risked troubling our friendship by identifying inconsistencies in his belief system.

The first issue was the suggestion that to be a critical thinker and a believer in the Bible were somehow mutually exclusive, somehow an impossible mix, they could not work.

The second inconsistency in his belief system was that the four Gospels were trustworthy but the Old Testament could not be trusted as God's Word.

Because of these two glaring fallacies, I asked him, "Have you ever read the Bible?" After shifting his eyes around and displaying uncharacteristic uncertainty in his demeanor he finally settled down and admitted that he had never really read the Bible all the way through. I assured him that it was not my intention to make him uncomfortable; but that I also considered myself a critical thinker and find the Bible to be overwhelmingly trustworthy. "We wouldn't be the first to be critical thinkers and believe in the credibility of the Bible. There are millions of people spanning generations and centuries who perfectly hold the two in balance," I assured him.

Old and New Testaments Complement Each Other

I continued to explain that it would be contradictory to believe in the four Gospels and simultaneously disbelieve the Old Testament since they are interconnected. Although the Old and New Testaments are complete works in themselves, the New Testament continues the story of man's fall and redemption, begun in the Old. The Old Testament gives us the origins of man, sin, the Jewish race, and the background of Jewish laws and customs. The New Testament, although complete, is benefitted greatly from the Old. It may be compared to watching a movie in black and white. But when read in light of the history, promises, and predictions of the

Old Testament, the New Testament comes alive in full Technicolor. The New Testament is a sequel to the Old Testament.

Jesus' claim to be the Son of God and the Christ (Anointed one or Messiah) is authenticated not only by His spotless life and miracles, but because He is the only possible fulfillment of hundreds of Old Testament prophecies:

He is the only one who was born of a virgin (Isaiah 7:14, Matthew 1:23, Luke 2:36)—thereby fulfilling the prophecy in the Old Testament.

He fulfilled Micah 5:2, which prophesied that the Messiah was to be born in Bethlehem.

John 19:37 relates that He also fulfilled Zachariah 12:10 which says,

They will look on Me whom they have pierced.

In the preceding verse, John 19:36, another prophecy is fulfilled by Jesus, that of Psalm 34:20,

He keeps all His bones, not one of them is broken.

This particular prophecy was fulfilled when the soldiers approached the three men on death row hanging upon their crucifixion crosses. The soldiers went around and broke the legs of the two criminals on either side of Jesus to hasten their deaths so that they would avoid defiling the holy day, but when they were about to break the legs of Christ, they saw that He was already dead and did not touch Him—thus fulfilling the prophetic psalm.

A list of Old Testament prophecies and their fulfillment is provided at the conclusion of this chapter.

The Sign of Jonah

One of my favorites is the incident involving the religious leaders asking Jesus for a sign or proof of His messiah-ship. His reply to them was that . . . the only sign He was about to give them was the sign of the prophet Jonah,

> As Jonah was three days and three nights in the belly of the fish, so will the Son of Man be three days and three nights in the heart of the earth.
> —Matthew 12:38-40

This is one of my favorites because of its significance. For one thing, it is one of Jesus' prophecies. He predicted His own death and resurrection. If that is not significant enough, He tied the central purpose for His visit to our planet—to pay for the sins of the world through His death—to one of the most disputed Old Testament narratives. Did He know there would be skeptics through all generations finding it difficult to believe that a man could be swallowed by a fish and regurgitated upon the shore? Without a doubt!

It was to this prophecy in Matthew that I turned when my colleague said that he believed in the Gospels but not the Old Testament. How could anyone believe the Gospels and Jesus while disbelieving the Old Testament and Jesus' endorsement of it? To believe one is to accept the other; they are interconnected.

IS JESUS LIAR, LUNATIC, OR LORD?

If the experience of Jonah is fabricated by men as some claim, then Jesus is a liar. If Jesus is a liar then He is a sinner. This would disqualify Him from paying for humanity's sins.

In his book, More Than A Carpenter, Josh McDowell wrote that Jesus may be one of three possibilities, Liar, Lunatic, or Lord. Not entirely original with him, McDowell built upon the argument of agnostic-turned-believer C. S. Lewis, who in his book Mere Christianity, answered those who dismissed Jesus as merely a great human teacher. Jesus cannot be what He claimed to be if what He said was found to be false. He would be a liar. Another possibility is that He genuinely believed He was who He said He was but He was out of His mind. He was a lunatic. A third possibility is that everything He said and did was true. In this case, we must accept Him for who He said He was which is Lord over all. Since Jesus words have come true, the evidence points to Jesus being Lord. Here are Lewis' words,

> A man who was merely a man and said the sort of things Jesus said would not be a great moral teacher. He would either be a lunatic—on the level with a man who says he is a poached egg—or he would be the devil of hell. You must take your choice. Either this was, and is, the Son of God, or else a madman or something worse. You can shut Him up for a fool or you can fall at His feet and call Him Lord and God. But let us not come with any patronizing nonsense about His being a great human teacher. He has not left that open to us (Lewis, 1960, p.40).

In the Bible, a prophet's word was held in very high regard. Because prophets spoke on God's behalf, they had to be extremely careful to say exactly what God gave them to say, not their own thoughts and feelings. According to Deuteronomy 18:20-22, there was no room for error in a prophet's prophecy. He had to be accurate 100% of the time.

Both their credibility and their life were at stake. So Jesus' claims about Himself were both unquestionable and verifiable. Lewis was absolutely right, Jesus has not left the option open to us that He was merely a great human teacher or just a good man; He claimed to be the Son of God.

Peter W. Stoner (1888-1980) authored his influential book, Science Speaks: Scientific Proof of the Accuracy of Prophecy and the Bible. Of the hundreds of Old Testament predictions about the Messiah, his birth, life, death, and resurrection, Stoner selected eight such predictions and initially studied the probability of one man fulfilling all eight of them. The question Stoner had been concerned with was: What is the chance that any man might have lived from the day of these prophecies down to the present time and have fulfilled all eight of these prophecies? The number he and his staff came up with was 1 in 10^{17} power or 1 in 100,000,000,000,000,000. Since this number is difficult to fathom, Stoner offered this word picture:

> Let us try to visualize this chance. If you mark one of ten tickets, and place all of the tickets in a hat, and thoroughly stir them, and then ask a blindfolded man to draw one, his chance of getting the right ticket is one in ten. Suppose that we take 10^{17} silver dollars and lay them on the face of Texas. They will cover all of the state two feet deep. Now mark one of these silver dollars and stir the whole mass thoroughly, all over the state. Blindfold a man and tell him that he can travel as far as he wishes, but he must pick up one silver dollar and say that this is the right one. What chance would he have of getting the right one? Just the same chance that the prophets would have had of writing these eight prophecies and having them all come true in

any one man, from their day to the present time, providing they wrote using their own wisdom (1969, p. 41).

These scientific evidences further support Jesus' claims to be the promised Messiah and the Son of God. It is precisely because of such compelling supporting evidence that one's faith is further informed. Jesus is the only person who fits all the prophecies about Messiah.

FULFILLED PROPHECIES

Our faith in the Bible's predictions of future events can rest firmly upon the pinpoint accuracy of already-fulfilled biblical prophecy. In other words, the fulfillment of biblical prophecies which are yet to be fulfilled may be anticipated with great confidence because of the previous fulfillment of other biblical predictions.

While Sarah, Abraham's wife, was both past childbearing age and barren, God told Abraham that he was going to have a son and he did. God told Abraham in Genesis 15: 13-16, that his descendants would be enslaved and oppressed for four hundred years and then be delivered from their captors. It was a prophecy which was fulfilled in Exodus 12: 40-41 just as God predicted. In Daniel 2: 31-45, Nebuchadnezzar, king of Babylon, had his dream interpreted by the prophet Daniel. That prophecy predicted the rise and fall of the then future Medio-Persian, Greek, and Roman Empires. History has borne out the ups and downs of those Empires just as they had been predicted to occur.

Because of these and countless already-fulfilled prophecies, we may have complete faith in the yet-to-be-fulfilled prophecies. All of the Bible's prophecies were fulfilled literally and we have no reason to believe that the predictions still future will not likewise be literally fulfilled.

The prophet himself was to be tested. He would demonstrate his genuineness (that he was commissioned by God) by making a prediction in the short-term. If the prophecy came true he was allowed to live and deemed genuine; if the prophecy failed however, he was considered a false prophet and was given the death penalty (see Deuteronomy 18: 20-22). These men spoke on behalf of God. The Almighty acted swiftly and severely upon false prophets who deceitfully prophesied in His name without His approval.

DIVINE INSPIRATION

The evidence for the inspiration and authority of the Bible cannot be ignored when considering its credibility. The most popular accusation leveled against the Bible's authenticity is probably that it was written by men. Accusers infer by this that it must therefore, be filled with errors, be biased, and certainly not authoritative. This common accusation however, is akin to the criticisms some heap upon countries and cultures they have neither studied nor visited. Many who express these sentiments never read the Bible. If they did they would have discovered that there is a dual authorship of the Bible. Both God and men coauthored the Holy Scriptures. More specifically, God inspired the human authors (2 Peter 1:20-21). The idea is that God guided the outcome of the Bible. The sinless, perfect God ensured that the original autographs were error free.

R. C. Sproul stated in his 1980 contribution, Explaining Inerrancy, that:

> Inerrancy is a corollary of inspiration inasmuch as it is unthinkable that God should inspire that which is fraudulent, false, or deceitful (p. 33).

The Bible's own claim to inspiration is found in the New Testament.

> All Scripture is inspired by God . . . .
> —2 Timothy 3:16

The Bible stands in its own defense. This self-witness is as valid as any person taking the witness stand in their own defense in a court of law. It is legitimate to do so.

JESUS DEFENDS THE OLD TESTAMENT

In the Gospels, Jesus more than any other person endorsed the credibility of the then canonized Scriptures, the Old Testament. In Matthew 5:17-18 He explained:

> Do you think I came to abolish the Law or the Prophets? I did not come to abolish, but to fulfill. For truly I say to you, until heaven and earth pass away, not the smallest letter or stroke shall pass away from the Law, until all is accomplished.

The Law and the Prophets comprise the entire Old Testament. All creation would sooner cease to exist before even one dotting of an "i" or crossing of a "t" in the Scriptures fail to come true. Everything written therein must be fulfilled.

Another clear and unmistakable example of Jesus' full approval of the Scriptures is recorded in Mark 7: 8-13. He was answering His critics when He said,

> Neglecting the *commandment of God*, you hold to the tradition of men. . . . You nicely set aside the *commandment of God* in order to keep your tradition. For *Moses said*, honor your father and your mother; and he who speaks evil of father or mother, let him be put to death; but you say, if a man says to his father or his mother, anything of mine you might have been helped by is Corban (that is to say, given to God), you no longer permit him to do anything for his father or his mother; thus invalidating *the Word of God* by your tradition which you have handed down; and you do many things such as that.

In this quote, there are three phrases (all in italics) Jesus uses which indicate that the Old Testament is Scripture and are, therefore, inspired by God. The first phrase is the expression, "commandment of God;" the second is, "Moses said," and the third is "the Word of God." These three show the dual authorship of Scripture. For, what *Moses said* was just as recognized and binding as the *commandment of God* and was referred to by Jesus as *the Word of God*. If we believe Jesus, we also believe this is God's Word.

This quote in Mark 7 was a direct affront to the Pharisees who were belittling the importance of the Old Testament Scriptures by replacing them with their own traditions just like my friend Thomas did.

OTHER FORMS OF INSPIRATION

It is important here to distinguish between biblical inspiration and other uses to the term inspiration. Biblical inspiration is different from say, musical inspiration or the inspiration one gets to compose a work of art. A freshly brewed cup of coffee has been known to provide inspiration for some to produce their impressive works. A timely and highly motivational speech can generate similar effect on some. Others have attributed to marijuana the inspiration for their compositions. But biblical inspiration is a more direct act of God. In fact, it is said to be God-breathed.

BIBLICAL AUTHORS—A DIFFERENT BREED

When composing autobiographical works, it is human nature to include and overstate those things which bring praise, admiration, and the approval of others. On the other hand, we tend to understate the things in our lives that might bring shame and are generally frowned upon in our culture. An interesting phenomenon occurred with the inspired biblical writers. Many of them told the whole truth about their lives, including the unpleasant episodes which can cast them in a bad light.

Moses, who wrote the first five books of the Bible and a few of the Psalms, included the murder he committed against an Egyptian when trying to defend a fellow Hebrew.

David, who was responsible for numerous chapters of the Psalms, referenced his infamous adultery with Bathsheba and subsequent cover-up attempts, which resulted in her husband Uriah's, murder.

The prophet Hosea documented his marriage to a prostitute.

The disciple Matthew, a tax collector for the Roman rulers was notorious for embezzling funds and overcharging his own countrymen. He chronicled this in his gospel.

The apostle Paul devoted his life to torturing and killing Christians prior to his conversion. He too tells all to inquiring minds in his epistles.

It is natural for us to want to keep private our dirty laundry and not expose them for all to see. Without God directing those authors we'd expect them to cover-up or omit these episodes from their accounts.

These and other witnesses occupy the witness stand in defense of the Bible's creditability. Collectively, they have withstood the test of time and endured countless onslaughts from rival belief systems. To this day, as throughout its history, the Bible is banned from some countries. It is burned daily in various parts of the world in efforts to silence its voice by some who feel threatened by its undeniable message. The Bible's authenticity is herein established. Thus, it is sensible and safe to apply an informed faith in its authority.

PROPHECIES ABOUT JESUS AND THEIR FULFILLMENT

Prophecy/Prediction	Old Testament Prediction	New Testament Fulfillment
He shall be born of a virgin	Isaiah 7:14	Matthew 1:22-23
He would be from the tribe of Judah	Genesis 49:10	Luke 3:23, 33
He would be born in Bethlehem	Micah 5:1-2	Matthew 2:1, 6; Luke 2:11
He would be of the Davidic line	Isaiah 9:6-7	Acts 13:22-33
He would have a forerunner	Isaiah 40:3	Matthew 3:1-2
He would be a miracle worker	Isaiah 35: 5-6	Matthew 9:35
He would appear in Jerusalem upon a donkey	Zechariah 9:9	Matthew 21: 6-11
He would be sold for 30 pieces of silver	Zechariah 11:12	Matthew 26:15; 27:1-8
He would be abandoned by His disciples	Zechariah 13:7	Matthew 14:20
He would be mute before His accusers	Isaiah 53:7	Matthew 27:12
He would be wounded and spat upon	Isaiah 50:6	Matthew 26:27
He would be pierced	Isaiah 53:5; Zechariah 12:10	John 19:34
There would be darkness over the land at midday	Amos 8:9	Matthew 27:45
No bones will be broken	Psalm 34:20	John 19:23
He would be offered gall and vinegar to drink	Psalm 69:21	Matthew 27:34
They would gamble for His garments	Psalm 22:18	John 19:23-24
He would question God's abandonment of Him	Psalm 22:1	Matthew 27:46
He would be crucified with criminals	Isaiah 53:12	Matthew 27:38
Money thrown in the Temple	Zechariah 11:13	Matthew 27:5
He would offer Himself as king of Israel	Daniel 9:26-27	Luke 19:41-44
He would be buried in a rich man's tomb	Isaiah 53:9	Matthew 27: 57-60
He would be from the tribe of Judah	Genesis 49:10	Luke 3:23, 33

CHAPTER 3 DISCUSSION QUESTIONS

1. What are some popular accusations against the Bible's credibility?

2. What gives the Bible credibility?

3. Why is Jesus' claim to be the Son of God a credible claim?

4. What role do already-fulfilled prophecies play in informed faith?

5. In what ways are biblical authors unique?

Chapter 4

Informed Faith Vs. Blind Faith

He who knows the road can ride full trot.
—Benjamin Franklin

lthough faith by nature requires trust, it is highly advisable that one's decision to believe comes after thorough investigation. People ought to be guarded when venturing into situations without absolute confidence. We are better off striving for an informed decision, an informed trust.

Our faith-o-meter gauges our degree of confidence in a given matter. At anytime our faith may grow, recede, strengthen, or weaken. Faith is not passive it's always active. It's not, did you believe? It's, do you believe? Faith does not happen to us, we choose to believe, trust, obey, be loyal, be persuaded, and have confidence. Faith may be cold, cool, warm, or hot. It is in a constant flow of change. Even when it is at rest, it is actively at rest trusting in God. There is a direct relationship between the degree to which we know something and our level of expected confidence. More knowledge, more confidence! Less knowledge, less confidence! In fact, it is precisely because of this knowledge-to-confidence ratio that people ought to learn as much as they can before pledging their support to any cause.

Look Before You Leap

Faith's nature is to commit, to be loyal, to place confidence in, to rest upon, and to trust. Because of its far-reaching ramifications and high risk (chapter seven discusses the risk involved in faith), this tendency requires thought and consideration; it requires thoughtfulness and fact-checking.

Not many loving fathers, for instance, are willing to risk their daughters' wellbeing by giving them away in marriage to men they know very little about. Because, the giving of one's heart is akin to committing one's trust. The potential for great happiness as well as great sorrow is companion to each decision to commit.

I have enjoyed the honor of witnessing couples pledge their love in holy matrimony. And I cannot recall a single occasion when I didn't hear these solemn and sobering words: Marriage is not, by any means, to be entered into unadvisedly or lightly. Why? Because the stakes are too high to naively trust. Our world is littered with examples of individuals, groups, and entire cultures of people who fail to heed this sensible warning.

Admittedly, we are not always punished for our failure to do our homework. Sometimes we trust in people, things, and ideas without the benefit of thorough investigation and remain quite satisfied with our choice. More often than not however, we endure grave consequences for our naïve choices. The risks are often too great to mindlessly entrust ourselves to causes, be they political, religious, cultural, or otherwise.

BIBLICAL EVIDENCE FOR INFORMED FAITH

The idea of arriving at a comfortable level of informed faith is not without strong biblical support despite criticism from skeptics that the Bible is a book to be taken on blind faith. "No thinking person" they say, "can take it seriously." They assume (wrongly) that all believers blindly trust God without any evidence upon which to base their faith.

But nothing could be further from the truth. God doesn't expect His creatures to switch off their brains and "rev-up" their emotions to blindly believe in Him. On the contrary, He anticipates that our decision to trust Him comes from our examination of His character, His works displayed in creation, His proven track record of fulfilling promises and prophecies, and the witness of His Spirit.

Evidence from God and Adam

Revisit the earliest record of man's interactions with God. Resist the inclination to think that God expected the first man to unquestionably obey Him when He mandated,

> From any tree of the garden you may eat freely; but from the tree of knowledge of good and evil you shall not eat, for in the day that you eat from it you shall surely die.
> —Genesis 2:16-17

On the surface it may appear that no opportunity was provided Adam to scrutinize God's ways to see if He was indeed worthy of his loyalty. But, the Genesis account informs us that the two shared ample time together. Before sin entered the picture, it appears Adam enjoyed occasional visits from God and spent time conversing with Him in the cool of the day.

God ensured that our first parents had access to overwhelming evidence and intimate knowledge of His character to make a viable judgment. Interestingly, nowhere are we told that the same opportunity was extended to them to observe the serpent at work; although, they may have had plenty of opportunity to observe that trickster too. Yet, with their limited knowledge they harkened unto the creature described as,

> More crafty than any beast of the field.
> —Genesis 3:1

To this day the human race is still in turmoil from that choice. So it is clear that God gave Adam ample opportunity to know His ways. He didn't expect a blind application of faith. Our first parents had the tools to make an informed decision to trust a benevolent God.

Evidence from Jesus and the Crowds

Jesus appeared on the scene claiming to be the Son of God. Now there is no greater claim than that of being GOD. How could He realistically expect people to believe Him? After all He looked like any other man. And yet, did He adopt the attitude which says, "Look! I know I am the Son of God; the Heavenly Father knows I am the Son of God; the angels know I am the Son of God, and I command you to believe Me! I don't have to prove Myself to you! Just believe that I am who I say I am!?" Absolutely not! Instead, He spent the last three years of His earthly life moving around one of earth's busiest metropolises providing everyone abundant opportunity to have His life and claims scrutinized as under a microscope. And scrutinized it was.

While on His visit to our planet, Jesus performed numerous miracles, fulfilled hundreds of prophecies, prophesied of future events, never contradicted Himself, never broke God's law, displayed kindness, gentleness, and grace to all including His enemies, taught the masses the things of God, refuted false teachings from the brightest minds of the time, voluntarily sacrificed His life for the world, rose from among the dead three days later, and was seen by more than 500 people at one time.

He engaged in numerous interchanges whereby His teachings about God and His claim to be the Son of God may be put to the test. He did not evade His enemies' scrutinizing attention and frequent interrogations; instead, He accommodated them.

On one occasion Paul, the apostle, stood trial before King Agrippa and concluded his defense of the life of Jesus by reminding the king,

> This has not been done in a corner.
>
> —Acts 26:26

They were done openly. Jesus' life, death, and resurrection were an open book. It afforded them every opportunity to an evidence-based faith, an informed faith.

The four Gospels are regarded as the primary records documenting His life on earth. And the Gospel of John was specifically written to provide evidence authenticating Jesus' claims to be the Son of God. Its stated purpose was to create faith within its readers. John explained that Jesus performed many other miracles in the presence of His disciples, which were not recorded in his book,

> But these have been written that you may believe that
> Jesus is the Christ, the Son of God; and that believing you
> may have life in His name.
>
> —John 20: 30

Jesus expects us to apply an informed faith in Him; He does not endorse blind faith. He validates and affirms the engagement of mindful thought to intelligently weigh the evidence and arrive at an informed decision.

Evidence from Malachi 3:10

Apart from carefully studying the character of the Holy One in history—Adam, observing God and the masses monitoring Jesus—God's integrity may still be examined today. In Malachi 3:10, God invited the people to test Him to see if He was true to His Word. Selah. Don't rush over those stunning words. Allow that thought to marinate in your mind and heart for a moment. The supreme God of heaven and earth has welcomed His creatures' examination of Him. Wow! Absolutely transparent and vulnerable! There is nothing to suggest that such an invitation was limited only to the believers of that time.

By the way, Jesus challenged His enemies, you heard right, His enemies, to do the same with Him; i.e. to examine Him for sin. The Jewish religious rulers of His day were setting traps to kill Him. Like salivating pit-bulls, the Scribes and Pharisees were constantly on the lookout for opportunity to sink their teeth into His divine jugular. Aware of their intentions, He offered them the chance to indict Him,

> Which one of you convicts Me of sin?
>
> —John 8:46

In other words, which of you can rightfully accuse Me of a single fault? None could. He was flawless. He was sinless.

Informed faith is not limited to biblical examples. When we accept God's challenge to prove Him, it informs our faith one way or the other. The testimony of innumerable believers down through the ages attests to a vibrant, experiential, evidence-based faith.

The essence of Malachi 3:10 is one of God lavishly providing and caring for the needs of all those who honor Him as God. But before He does, He sets a condition. Here is His invitation:

> "Bring what belongs to Me into My storehouse so that there may be food in My house and prove me now," says the Lord of hosts "And see if I will not open for you the windows of heaven, and pour out for you a blessing until it overflows."
>
> —Malachi 3:10

This meant that the people were to pay a tenth of their farm yield and sacrifice the firstborn of the animals. The idea is simple. As our creator, provider, and protector, God must be honored as God. He must be given His rightful place in our lives. When that is done, this promise may be tested. The Proverbs put it this way,

> Honor the Lord from your wealth
> And from the first of all your produce;
> So your barns will be filled with plenty
> And your vats will overflow with new wine.
> —Proverbs 3:9-10

We can examine God's reputation, His track record and His ability to deliver what He promised, after we've gotten the relationship right—that He is God and we are His creatures. He is to be worshiped. We must obey His commandments, submit our wills to His, and genuinely love Him, not merely say that we do. This means our pocketbooks and wallets may not be withheld from His reach. A comprehensive and purposeful giving of one's self is in view here. This is a tall order; but, not an unreasonable one. It is the essence of faith.

When this decision to put God first is in operation, one can expect to have the full blessing and favor of God. Within a reasonable time frame, we may appraise the value of God's promise. Why does He require all this? Well, He is God! He fully deserves all His creatures' reverence, worship, and trust. Not only that, but God has placed His reputation on the line by statements such as those made in Malachi 3:10. Like anything else however, we must get the whole equation right. We must give Him first place in our lives then we may expect the promised blessings. Countless believers who lived this way have proven God to be faithful to His promises.

AMY'S PROVEN FAITH

Amy's story exemplifies the millions of believers around the world who have proven God's Word to be trustworthy.

This tiny woman stands five-feet tall, possessing nothing much beyond her relentless faith in Jesus Christ. She insists that without Christ she amounts to nothing. By the way, this is true of us all. Amy is fortunate enough to recognize and acknowledge it. With an absentee husband deserting her with twelve children to care for all by herself, Amy encountered countless opportunities to prove whether God was trustworthy. Without a husband to provide and protect her and the children, opportunist men launched constant threats to take advantage of her vulnerable status. But she refused to give in to their empty promises; instead, she looked to God whom she proved over and over again. How do you care for a dozen children with a working class salary? One of her favorite Scriptures to which she clung confirmed God's faithfulness,

> I have been young, and now I am old; yet I have not seen the righteous forsaken nor his descendants begging bread.
> —Psalms 37:25

These and other Scriptures were ever-present upon her lips, spoken both in times when she needed reassurance that things were going to be alright and during times of boasting about God's providence.

Although there were times of financial hardships, there were never occasions when she had to be fearful of law enforcement authorities or when her children went to bed without a proper meal. The boys enjoyed sports and played games with each other and neighboring friends. The girls also enjoyed childhood games among neighboring company. Most of her kids were afforded a high school education. Some of them benefited from a college education all the way through graduate school. And the promised blessings spoken of in Malachi 3:10, continues to flow.

Today Amy enjoys good health and is content to live comfortably around her children. Her daily habit of praying for her family has not been abandoned. She credits God for her sustenance and overall good fortune. Hers' is an informed faith. It is not for a lack of options that she believes in Jesus Christ; but, because she's proven Him over and over again.

She relates episode after episode accounting for God as the only possible explanation for her sustenance and preservation today.

Amy and the Letter

Amy described an incident in which the only feasible explanation was God's timely providence during a time of great need. The tone and energy of her voice while telling the story was reminiscent of over-comers. Her certainty of God's nearness and her undeniable love for her offspring may explain the strong emotions evident in her expressions. The three-bedroom quaint abode they called home was neatly tucked away in the western part of a Caribbean island. With two of her children already making their homes in far-away America, the local occupancy now shrunk to eleven—Amy and her ten other kids.

She remembers a day when all her resources were spent. Now, there are times when many families go through a rough patch financially. As for Amy, she could always find something to prepare for the kids. This time however, she could find nothing to put before her family. The kitchen garden had yet to produce a yield that summer. There was nothing, absolutely nothing with which to feed her household. Sitting on the front stoop with her overworked, tiny hands propping up her chin, she was worried about providing food for her family.

Amy took her need to God in prayer and waited. Minutes seemed like hours as the twilight slowly chased away the remaining daylight when one of her kids approached with singing on her lips. Oblivious to her mother's plight, yet noticing her defeated posture, she blurted out in her colorful Caribbean accent,

Mammy, why are you looking so downhearted? Trust in the Lord! Has He ever let you down before?

Not knowing the full magnitude of her words toward the grave situation Amy was up against; she produced a letter which arrived from the States that day. As Amy tore open the welcomed interruption, the answer to her prayers was nestled neatly inside the overseas correspondence. A stack of cash lovingly lay within. Deployed some two weeks earlier, the valuable mail arrived at its intended destination not a moment too soon. It was valuable in more ways than one—it allowed Amy to purchase much needed food, and it proved once again that God was true to His Word. Because the American currency was stronger than the Caribbean currency, the amount of cash would be more than enough in those days to buy sufficient food for quite some time.

Although skeptics may offer alternative explanations, Amy cannot with clear conscience attribute the timing and content of that envelope to coincidence or any other factor. There is no other rationale than that it was God's answer to her prayers and her faith in Him. Many such experiences, especially after deciding to approach God in prayer confirms God's clear hand of providence. Amy's faith is not one which is blind. It has been tested and proven. Her belief in God results from repeated experiences like these where she had victories over disparaging threats. These all conspire to inform her faith. She trusted and obeyed Him by putting Him first in her life. Watchman Nee, the well-known Chinese Christian writer was insightful when he said,

True knowledge comes from obedience everything else is just information.

Amy and countless believers who obey God have proven Him and acquired true knowledge of God thus informing their faith in Him.

Please indulge me as I turn to the poets who have been blessed with insight and grace to capture the sentiments of our hearts. This piece by Edward Mote, who in 1834 composed the timeless hymn, The Solid Rock, is one of Amy's favorites. In it he declares with boldness where his faith is placed in contrast to other options he describes as quicksand. Every line may be studied to appreciate the depths of these words.

My hope is built on nothing less
Than Jesus' blood and righteousness;
I dare not trust the sweetest frame,
But wholly lean on Jesus' name.

Refrain:

On Christ, the solid Rock, I stand;
All other ground is sinking sand,
All other ground is sinking sand.

When darkness veils His lovely face,
I rest on His unchanging grace;
In every high and stormy gale,
My anchor holds within the veil.

His oath, His covenant, His blood
Support me in the whelming flood;

When all around my soul gives way,
He then is all my hope and stay.

When He shall come with trumpet sound,
Oh, may I then in Him be found;
Dressed in His righteousness alone,
Faultless to stand before the throne.

Informed faith breathes confidence into believers, assuring them that their trust has a basis in reason. As that daughter confidently reminded Amy—*has He ever let you down before?*

After seekers and skeptics have explored every question, exhausted every argument, expressed every uncertainty and thoroughly examined every avenue available to them, a torrent of self-assurance saturates the mind when they finally turn to God. Buoyancy, excitement, happiness, peace, assurance, and conviction characterize those who appropriate informed trust. A measure of integrity and affirmation accompanies knowledgeable trust and creates satisfaction in most.

DANGERS OF BLIND FAITH

Blind, unproven faith, on the other hand, tends to lack certainty and integrity. The object upon which one places blind faith may or may not be worthy of their trust. Whatever reasons people fail to investigate a matter before committing their trust—be it laziness, a naïve appraisal of its nature, a nonchalant approach to life, or pressure from an authority figure in one's life—it is always an ill-advised practice. The exercise of blind faith does not reflect mature and responsible behavior. And although stalwarts may not outwardly relent from their uninformed but stubborn stance, within them the fear-of-failure lurks as a constant, nagging possibility. As much as they try to suppress and deny it to themselves, they instinctively know that they stand on shaky ground. Like the troubled sea, there is continual unrest.

Domain of Demagogues

In fact this tendency in some plays dangerously into the hands of demagogues who pounce upon the unquestioned loyalties of their followers. The world has produced countless examples of blind faith—the naïve pledging their loyalty to persons and causes after only minimum investigation or no investigation at all.

Communist North Korea, Cuba, and to a lesser extent China cannot deny their Governments' interference and control over their citizens' beliefs. Their masses are not free to believe what they desire; the State indoctrinates them with its brand of propaganda. Outside religions are considered threats to their particular method of leadership. They demand absolute control of their citizens' minds. Even as these words are being typed, I received word, from a colleague visiting a Middle Eastern country, who expressed frustration that internet access to a western television stream had been blocked. He wanted merely to view his favorite football team take on their arch rival. These countries promote blind faith; they discourage all attempts to investigate other options.

Religious cults find themselves at the forefront of these ploys. The most detrimental characteristic common among these groups is their leaders' unquestioned authority linking them in some mystical way to God. Since leaders of these cultic groups bully their authority upon followers as a God-given directive, they expect unquestioned faith and loyalty from members.

It is this feature more than any other, which stands in sharp contrast to biblical Christianity. Christ and Christianity encourage informed trust. Not unlike the popular SYMS® television commercial which announces, "An educated consumer is our best customer." Similarly, among God's best believers are informed believers.

The apostle Peter, aware of the dangers blind-faith leaders pose, urged Christians to always be ready to provide a reason for their faith (1 Peter 3:15); unfortunately, many uninformed believers are unable to do so.

FAITH AND REASON—A GOOD MARRIAGE

Where there is reluctance to wed faith with reason, it may be retraced to a bygone era beginning in the 18th century when Christians reacted to the emergence of science. During that time, there was a large-scale transfer of belief in God to belief in science. Darwin's theory of evolution in particular culminated in the infamous Scopes Trial. Also known as the Monkey Trial and The Trial of The Century, John T. Scopes, a substitute biology teacher, advocated the teaching of the evolutionary theory in schools. The State, represented by William Jennings Bryan, defended the right to keep on teaching the Bible's creation account in schools. How could this happen? Did the Christians of that period possess a faith which was grounded in thought? Was their faith built upon superstitions? Was their faith a blind faith? Or did they believe based on some other set of evidences? No doubt a combination of these accounted for the reasons they believed. Faith and reason need not be mutually exclusive;

they work best when they coexist together. They do not oppose each other. On the contrary, they support each other.

Some Christians resist new ideas without the benefit of fully examining them. Their unfounded fears sway them to slam the door on reason. But this tendency to prejudge ideas which appear to pose a danger to fundamental tenets of one's beliefs is not unique to Christians. It is a particularly human defense mechanism.

Nevertheless as we have seen, informed faith enjoys the support of the holy Bible. If Christians believe they possess the truth, there should be absolutely no reason for panic. Truth will always emerge triumphant. It does not need to be defended; it is its own defense. Truth is like cork; no matter how many times you try to sink it, it will always rise to the top. It is unshakable. When Christians feel particularly defensive and insecure about their faith, it may indicate symptoms of uninformed belief. Because informed faith tends to bolster believers' confidence.

Moreover, Christians need not feel threatened by the theory of evolution since such an explanation for our existence requires more faith than it would take to believe in the Bible's creation account. By the way, this may be a good place to remind ourselves that the theory of evolution is just that—a theory. It is an unproven supposition, a claim, a hypothesis. The creation account is revelation from God through His inspired word.

The amount of faith needed to believe that millions of years ago the planets *happened* to all align themselves and the conditions *happened* to be just right for life to begin, constitute a huge leap of faith—blind faith. Where did the planets come from in the first place? Did they just *happen* out of nowhere too? God is the only uncaused entity. He alone provides the best explanation for the existence of everything else. To many, the leap of faith is significantly smaller and supported with wholesome reason when asked to believe that there was a mastermind behind the creation of the world.

On its own, order does not result from disorder. And that is what we are being asked to believe with the theory of evolution. The parts of a wrist watch, for instance, will not fall into place and begin to work no matter how long or how many times they are randomly thrown together. No condition may be just right for them to line up and begin to work on their own. As with the universe, someone had to conceive of it, create it, and put it together. There had to be a designer. And our designer is God.

&

CHAPTER 4 DISCUSSION QUESTIONS

1. What are some dangers of blind faith?

2. What are some evidences for informed faith?

3. What is the relationship between faith and reason?

Chapter 5

The Reasonableness of Faith

For as the heavens are higher than the earth,
so are My ways higher than your ways
and My thoughts than your thoughts.

—Isaiah 55:9

FAITH—A COMMON EXPERIENCE

Whether we are aware of it or not, everyone exercises faith every day. In many ways and situations we put our trust in people and things all the time. If truth be told, we cannot, not exercise faith. From infancy through adulthood, faith is companion to life as we know it.

Newborns exercise faith in their parents. They trust their mothers for food, clothing, shelter, security, and love; they are totally vulnerable and dependent. Dependent! There is another synonym for faith.

Adults place confidence in their own abilities to do their jobs and to provide for their families. We trust that the air we breathe contains enough oxygen to sustain us so-much-so that most never give the complexity of breathing a thought. We all believe in the ability of the chairs we sit on and the beds we sleep on to bear our weight. When we climb the stairs of an aircraft, we relinquish all control to the pilot (whom most never meet), place confidence in its engineers to produce a reliable product that will become airborne and remain suspended in air for hours, and safely land us in our places of destiny. When we flip on a light-switch we believe the room will be brightened. Most believe their brand-new cars will transport them to and from desired locations. Many trust that their jobs, bank accounts, and financial portfolios will provide them a sense of financial security.

The fact is everyone lives by some measure of faith; it is a reality we cannot escape. We place our confidence in people and things every day. The exercise of faith is among the most normal of things we do moment by moment. It is so natural that most do not realize they are indeed practicing faith.

One of faith's interesting peculiarities is that it is crucial to meaningful relationships. Ask almost anyone what they consider most important to a thriving relationship and their first answer will almost always be trust. As we know, trust is a synonym of faith. The words may be used interchangeably. And it is a major building block, the cornerstone of positive, healthy relationships. Of course, this is not limited to the intimacy shared in marital relationships; this indispensable trait is central to the parent-child bond as well. And fiduciary trust demands to be foremost among persons in a business agreement. Siblings, friends, choir members, coworkers, and teammates all depend upon their trust in each other to be the adhesive that keeps them from dismantling. We have a deep-seated need to trust and to be trusted. The enemy infidelity, like a bull in a China shop, poses a direct threat to the very survival of the relationship.

BECAUSE WE ARE FINITE

The reasonableness of faith is evident when we acknowledge that, apart from God, no one knows everything about anything. Therefore what we do not know in any given matter compels us to exercise faith. We usually gain confidence from the partial knowledge we possess. We reason that the rest which we do not know must likewise be of similar substance to that which we already know. Or, our inner voice assures us that the rest which are yet unknown are somehow safe and therefore trustworthy. We are really left with no other option; for, as was already established, no one knows everything about anything.

When farmers sow seeds in the field, they do not necessarily know much of what is responsible for them to produce a yield. They sow in faith like the rest of us. Sure, they may understand that seeds need a certain texture of soil, that they need to be watered, and that it would not hurt to be exposed to sunlight and oxygen. But that may be the extent of their knowledge. Do they understand exactly how a dry seed springs to life when conditions are favorable? They have to exercise faith. They must trust the process despite their limited knowledge. Even king Solomon, the wisest man who ever lived, acknowledged the activity of God, admitting his knowledge can only go so far and no farther. Solomon said,

> Just as you do not know the path of the wind and how bones are formed in the womb of a pregnant woman, so you do not know the activity of God who makes all things.
> —Ecclesiastes 11:5

Most people develop a measure of comfort with everyday things; they don't worry about the details for which they have no definite explanation. For instance, no one understands everything about the foods we eat. We trust that such delicacies are good for us since we have not been harmed by them. So our faith is based on our history with the foods we eat.

Job had his blurry vision cleared after an encounter with God. He found himself in extreme dire circumstances; so, he went on the attack and bombarded God with a barrage of questions. It was in the thirty-eighth chapter of the biblical book which bears his name that the Transcendent One finally spoke.

> Then the LORD answered Job out of a whirlwind:
> Who is this who darkens counsel with words without knowledge?
> Get ready for a difficult task like a man; I will question you and you will inform me!
> Where were you when I laid the foundation of the earth? Tell me if you possess understanding! Who set its measurements—if you know—or who stretched a measuring line across it? . . .
> Who shut up the sea with doors when it burst forth, coming out of the womb . . . when I prescribed its limits, and set in place its bars and doors, when I said, 'To here you may come and no farther, here your proud waves will be confined'?. . .
> In what direction does light reside, and darkness, where is its place, that you may take them to their borders and perceive the pathways to their homes?
> —Job 38:1-20

Read the whole fascinating account in Job 38-42. When Job finally caught his breath, his response was telling. Like most of us when we realize we've spoken out-of-turn or that we're in-over-our-heads, he confessed:

> I have declared without understanding things too
> wonderful for me to know.
>
> —Job 42:3

Truth be told, too often we speak about things we really don't understand. How could we truly understand? We are mere mortals, finite human beings. Faith, therefore, is a necessity.

BECAUSE GOD IS INFINITE

It is not surprising that faith is God's chosen vehicle to meaningfully engage the human race. Actually, it is quite plausible. I have always been enthralled with God's infinite vastness and the countless number of options available to Him. When it comes to choices, with Him the possibilities are endless. Nike Inc., the global sportswear giant, used extensively in one of their advertising campaigns the slogan, "Impossible Is Nothing." Such disregard for the extremely difficult and intolerance for excuses reflect the lofty ambitions of an overachieving corporation. But this motto can truly and literally apply only to God; because, to Him impossible does not exist. The boundaries set by Him in nature, He may transcend at any moment. How does He arrive at His choices?

For instance, in the mind of The Omniscient, there must have been an unlimited number of solutions to the problem of sin in the world; yet, God chose as a remedy the death of His Son. Why? Of course God does not always provide an explanation for His actions. He is not obligated to do so. We may not fully understand it if He did. After all, He is God; He knows and understands things we cannot fully comprehend. Hence faith emerged as a necessity.

Jesus' agonizing cry in the Garden of Gethsemane in the face of His impending crucifixion solemnly bears witness to this truth:

> "Father," He prayed, "If it is possible, let this cup pass from Me; yet not as I will, but as Thou wilt."
>
> —Luke 22:42

Even the Son of God sought a different option; but, the Father prized the option of His Son's death as the best solution. How much more must we as imperfect, fallen creatures depend upon the perfect, All Knowing One?

There exists a vast gap between God and man in every conceivable way. He is spirit; we are matter. He is omnipresent; we are confined to occupy one space at a time. He is omniscient; our knowledge is so limited that no one knows everything about anything. He is omnipotent; we do not even have control over how long we will live. How do we begin to bridge the gap? God is transcendent; He transcends everything else, He easily transcends us. He is infinite.

BECAUSE FAITH IS THE GREAT EQUALIZER

Since God is love, gracious, kind, merciful, just, patient, and long-suffering to name a few of His better known attributes, what are some reasonable considerations for faith as the preferred bridge between God and humankind?

Human access to God needed to be universal. That is, each person on the planet should have easy membership access. A child anywhere must intuitively comprehend enough and be free to obtain acceptance with God. Boundaries limiting anyone from having access to Him should not exist. Contact with God needed to be barrier-free. There should be no cultural barriers preventing us access to our Creator. Racial or ethnic boundaries ought not to exist when it comes to reaching the Almighty. There should not be any caste systems complicating one's path to the Supreme Judge. Economic hurdles should not threaten to block admission to God's presence. Language should not be an impediment to reaching God. One's level of education should not limit the frontiers of contact with the Omniscient One. One's gender should not be a liability; neither should it obstruct anyone from approaching the God of diversity. Even one's morality should not initially barricade seekers of the Holy One.

Whatever conduit God elected to bridge the domains between Him and us needed to be user-friendly. There should be no barriers at all. Meaningful contact with God also needed to be accessible; by this, I mean easy, not complicated. Access to Him must also provide integrity. It must not be deceptive. Rather it must be verifiable and provide confirmation when admission is granted. It should not be guess-work, and riddled with uncertainty.

Faith is the perfect medium by which all these criteria are satisfied. Everyone, from every conceivable walk of life whether rich or poor, educated or uneducated, healthy or unhealthy, good or bad, tall or short, black or white, male or female, socially prominent or socially marginal, can all exercise faith. Faith is no respecter of persons; it does not discriminate. It is the great equalizer; everyone finds equal footing in faith. It stands as the most reasonable means God could have provided to facilitate a meaningful relationship with humankind.

BECAUSE GOD IS A CONSUMING FIRE

Could you imagine what would happen if God appeared before us unveiled having absolutely no covering at all? Well we do not have to imagine. The Scriptures have drawn back the curtains to give us a glimpse into this rare occurrence.

Exodus 19 gives us some idea of what it would be like if God were to do just that. It documents a dramatic event after God delivered the children of Israel from 430 years of slavery in Egypt. En route to the Promised Land, the wandering band of Israelites grew impatient with Moses' leadership and launched a barrage of complaints. They were sick and tired with God's appointed leader; therefore, they were sick and tired with God. So how does the Almighty deal with this situation? He decided to pay them a personal visit.

Keep in mind that this is God we are talking about, not an angel, not a prophet, but God; this appearance is a personal visit by God Himself. But wait a minute! Hold on just a second! Am I reading right? You just don't casually stroll into the presence of God! So, what does the Almighty do? He instructed Moses to prepare the people for His arrival by having them consecrate themselves. They were to avoid anything considered ceremonially unclean; for, the Holy One was about to make an appearance. Mount Sinai was the chosen meeting place. No person or animal was to approach the base of the mountain lest they die. Why? The white hot purity of God's holiness would literally cremate anything containing a speck of defilement. The appointed time arrived and God was approaching.

The epic event described here reveals the reasonableness of faith in light of who God is:

> After Moses had gone down the mountain to the people, he consecrated them, and they washed their clothes.
>
> Then he said to the people, "Prepare yourselves for the third day. Abstain from sexual relations." On the morning of the third day there was thunder and lightning, with a thick cloud over the mountain, and a very loud trumpet blast. Everyone in the camp trembled. Then Moses led the people out of the camp to meet with God, and they stood at the foot of the mountain. *Mount Sinai was covered with smoke, because the LORD descended on it in fire. The smoke billowed up from it like smoke from a furnace, the whole mountain trembled violently, and the sound of the trumpet grew louder and louder.* Then Moses spoke and the voice of God answered him. *The LORD descended to the top of Mount Sinai and called Moses to the top of the mountain.* So Moses went up and the LORD said to him, "Go down and warn the people so they do not force their way through to see the LORD and many of them perish. Even the priests, who approach the LORD, must consecrate themselves, or the LORD will break out against them." Moses said to the LORD, "The people cannot come up Mount Sinai, because you yourself warned us, 'Put limits around the mountain and set it apart as holy.' "The LORD replied, "Go down and bring Aaron up with you. But the priests and the people must not force their way through to come up to the LORD, or he will break out against them."
>
> —Exodus 19:14-24

God cannot appear before us in all His glory lest we die. He is a consuming fire. He will cremate us. He usually veils His fullness when He shows up in the company of people. He shrouds His deity (sometimes in humanity) out of protective love for us as evidenced in Jesus Christ.

In the New Testament Jesus Christ appeared before us draped in a human body. Notice the words the prophet uses to capture Jesus' eternal existence and His timely incarnation.

> For a *Child* will be *born* to us, and a *Son* will be *given* to us.
> —Isaiah 9:6

The casual reader may miss the significance of the prophet's careful use of the words "Child born" and "Son given." As the Son given, the prophet points to Christ's deity. It references His pre-existence—this given Son always existed. The Son was not born; He always was. Whereas, the Child who will be born is the same person but references His appearance clothed in human flesh during a brief (33 years) slice of time.

John was more direct when he presented this amazing revelation to his readers. In chapter one of his Gospel he explained that God became flesh and dwelt among us.

> In the beginning was the Word, and the Word was with God, and *the Word was God.* . . All things were made by Him, and apart from Him nothing came into being that has come into being . . . And *the Word became flesh and lived among us*, and we beheld His glory, the glory as of the only begotten from the Father, full of grace and truth.
> —John1:1-14

It is reasonable therefore, that God chose faith as a means to communicate with us on a regular basis. We are finite; He is infinite. Faith is the great equalizer; it provides all of humanity fair and common ground to access Him. And He is a consuming fire; His holy nature will annihilate us. For, we are unfit in our current sinful condition to stand before Him; exposure to His unveiled presence will consume us. God transcends us; we need faith. He is just too big for us.

CHAPTER 5 DISCUSSION QUESTIONS

1. Do modern societies believe a life of faith is reasonable?

2. In what way(s) is faith a common experience for all?

3. How would God being infinite and humankind being finite make faith reasonable?

4. How does faith being the great equalizer make it reasonable?

5. How does God being a consuming fire make faith reasonable?

Chapter 6

The Simplicity of Faith
The Complexity of Believing

The great act of faith is when man decides that he is not God.
—Oliver Wendell Holmes

People all over the world find it difficult to believe that faith in Jesus Christ is God's sole requirement when granting eternal life to anyone. Something within us rejects the notion that the avenue to heaven could actually be that simple. Is faith all God requires? Is it really that simple? Yes! It is. And no! It is not. Let me explain. Yes! The Bible contains an embarrassment-of-riches concerning this teaching—John 3:16, John 5:24, John 14:1, Acts 16:31, Romans 5:1, and Ephesians 2:8-9 to list a few references. With a collective voice, it speaks with unrestrained unity on the subject. A brief glance at three Scripture verses provides ample evidence on this important matter.

FAITH'S SIMPLICITY—JOHN 5:24

In John 5:24, Jesus addressed religious leaders who had been challenging His claim to be the Son of God. He had recently cured a man who was sick for thirty-eight years. When the religious rulers learned the man had been made well, they interrogated him about the source of his healing. His attempts to inform them that it was Jesus who miraculously healed him, brought a death sentence upon Jesus because the healing occurred on a holy day. At least that's the excuse His would-be executioners used. Jesus' words further angered the religious clerics who intensified their determination to put Him to death. In John 5:17, Jesus explained,

> My Father is working until now, and I Myself am working.

At this, they picked up stones to throw at Him.

Why were the Jewish leaders so enraged to the point of murdering Him? Because they understood that Jesus was claiming to be God. John tells his readers,

> For this cause therefore, the Jews were seeking all the more to kill Him, because He not only was breaking the Sabbath, but also was calling God His own Father, making Himself equal with God.
>
> —John 5:18

This action by the religious leaders wouldn't have been so bad if any other person had been making the claims Jesus was making. Under Jewish law it would have been blasphemy which is punishable by stoning to death (see Leviticus 24:16). But Jesus provided irrefutable evidence which corroborated His claims—His perfect life, His many miracles, His persuasive words. It was during a lengthy reply to this that Jesus said,

> Truly, truly, I say unto you, he who hears My word, and believes Him who sent Me, has eternal life, and does not come into judgment, but has passed out of death into life.
>
> —John 5:24

Notice the synonym for faith? Believe. Here the sole requirement for receiving everlasting life is faith in God. The simplicity of exercising faith alone after one hears God's Word guarantees everlasting life, avoids God's judgment, and transfers one from the realm of death to the realm of life. Examine it closely for yourself.

FAITH'S SIMPLICITY—JOHN 3:16

John 3:16 is regarded by many as the Bible's central text, it reads,

> For God so loved the world, that He gave His only begotten (unique) Son, that whoever believes in Him should not perish, but have eternal life.

It was part of the conversation Jesus had with Nicodemus the ruler of the Jews. This ruler-ship Nicodemus exercised was more religious than it was political. A very religious man, he had been trained in all the traditions, customs, and precepts of God's Law. If Jesus wanted to pick a representative who should know the way to heaven, we would expect Nicodemus to be the ideal candidate. It so happened however, that it was Nicodemus who approached Jesus and opened the conversation with an acknowledgement of Jesus' obvious connection to God.

> Rabbi we know that You have come from God as a teacher; for no one can do these signs (miracles) You do unless God is with him.
>
> —John 3:2

Jesus chose not to respond to that comment seeing that He was more than just a teacher who came from God. Instead, He cut to the chase and brought up the spiritual miracle that needs to happen to anyone who aspires to see the kingdom of Heaven. Getting to heaven does not happen by being religious but by spiritual birth through the agency of faith. So Jesus told him,

> Truly, truly, I say to you, unless one is born again, he cannot see the kingdom of God.
>
> —John 3:3

This confused Nicodemus, who sought clarification,

> How can a man be born when he is old? He cannot enter a second time into his mother's womb and be born, can he?
>
> —John 3:4

Jesus explained that He was not referring to a physical birth but one that came from heaven. He clarified His point by mentioning a familiar incident found in the biblical book of Numbers 21:4-9. Since Nicodemus was trained in the Jewish Law, he would be familiar with this reference. In that narrative, the Israelites whined against God and His appointed leader, Moses who captained them through a wilderness to a divinely promised land. According to them, God was not providing food and water at their convenience. Their childish complaining tantrums invoked God's fatherly discipline upon them because He repeatedly provided all their needs, not necessarily their conveniences and desires. In a decisive move of judgment, God sent venomous serpents among them resulting in the death of some in the camp.

God's rescue operation was simple. Since the trespass had to do with their lack of faith in God as their provider, the remedy would require a restoration of their faith. Moses was to hoist a bronze serpent upon a pole in plain sight for all the wounded to see. There was only one requirement. The victims must look at the bronze serpent. It really was that simple. There was no additional requirement; nothing difficult, simply look at the remedy God provided. This action would distinguish those who believed in God from those who did not. For, a bronze serpent elevated upon a pole doesn't possess any known medicinal quality by which people may be cured from fatal snake bites. It was a look of faith in God. This is the setting from which the beloved and cherished text, John 3:16, emerges. To introduce it Jesus referred to a historical scene in the Law of Moses,

As Moses lifted up the serpent in the wilderness, even so must the Son of Man be lifted up; that whoever believes may in Him have eternal life.

—John 3:14-15

Keep in mind that Jesus engaged in this dialogue with a religiously astute man. Nicodemus was the appointed teacher of Israel. Jesus' immediate concern was to correct the universal misconception that good, religious observance is the way to heaven. Jesus attacked this erroneous belief by teaching about the necessity of a spiritual birth. To receive this heavenly birth people must exercise faith, nothing else. He reminded Nicodemus of the incident recorded in Numbers 21 to illustrate how one receives the remedy. As the snake-bitten Israelites looked at the bronze serpent for deliverance; so must the sinner look to God for His remedy for sins. According to John 3:16, the single requirement for acquiring everlasting life is faith in the Son of God—nothing else. Read it again,

> For God so loved the world, that He gave His only begotten (unique) Son that whoever *believes* in Him should not perish but have everlasting life.

FAITH'S SIMPLICITY—EPHESIANS 2:8-9

Ephesians 2:8-9 speaks to the simple requirement of faith in the spiritual equation that produces spiritual and eternal salvation. Paul, an apostle (specially sent one) of Jesus Christ, wrote to the church in the ancient city of Ephesus. In chapter two, Paul particularly wrote about God's great kindness to undeserving humankind in light of their equally great spiritual and moral bankruptcy. The members of that congregation were described as dead in trespasses and sins in which they once walked (lived) according to the ways of this world (2:1). But, that was a description of their past condition. Paul is now occupied with explaining both their current redeemed condition and how they arrived there. Let us look at this Scripture together. The underlined words are further explained in parenthesis. Ephesians 2:8 & 9,

> *For by grace* (God's unearned favor and kindness)
> *you have been saved* (delivered from eternal judgment)
> *through faith,* (placing your trust in Him)
> *And that not of yourselves* (not because of your goodness);
> *it is the gift of God* (kindness and the unearned present),
> *not of works* (any effort to contribute to your salvation),
> *so that no one can boast* (take credit for their own salvation).

People are saved (delivered from everlasting judgment) because of God's grace (unearned favor and kindness) towards them. His only requirement is still *faith* in Him. No amount of works or good deeds will, in anyway, contribute to a person's salvation. No one can take credit for getting to heaven. Salvation is all from God. Our sole requirement is to receive the gift of salvation by faith.

At one time Jesus taught His audience that unless they became like little children, they could not enter the kingdom of heaven. That was a pronouncement of simplicity. His point? The type of faith needed was so simple, it was like the type little children place in their parents and those to whom they are entrusted. They simply just trust.

It is common knowledge among Christian ministers that 85 percent of all people who believe in Christ do so before age 14. That type of faith could be exercised without one's conscience being corrupted by the debris of the world's anti-God philosophy.

NEED TO CONTRIBUTE COMPLICATES BELIEF

But if it is that simple to gain eternal life, why do so many fail to believe in Jesus? Why is it sometimes hard to exercise faith? Interestingly, that which makes it simple, may also account for what makes it complicated. Placing confidence in the sacrifice of a sinless man to turn away God's righteous anger is easy enough when we are convinced that it is the right way. The difficulty lies in the fact that any contribution of our own is unwelcome. It is rejected by God, and for good reason as we have already seen. As Ephesians 2:9 emphatically stated, the salvation of the Christians at the church of Ephesus was . . ."Not of works, so that none can boast." And generally speaking, the human race has a problem with that.

The struggles of an old man's heart expose the tensions experienced universally by many when faced with the exercise of simple faith.

The Missionary and the Old Man

The story is told of a missionary who became great friends with an old man in India where he served for several years. He had been trying to persuade the aging man to accept God's gift of eternal life simply by believing in Jesus Christ for the forgiveness of his sins. But the old man always had the same answer; it is too easy, it is too simple! It bothered him that all it required to be forgiven and inherit a peaceful eternity in heaven was to simply believe, nothing else.

Now, the elderly man lived near the ocean and often went diving for pearls. One day, when he and his missionary friend were discussing his latest find, he helped him to better appreciate the finer qualities of pearls. He pointed out the various shapes and imperfections which can devalue otherwise perfect pearls. The pair enjoyed a special friendship. But it was on a day when the old man thought he might be seeing his missionary friend for the last time that he shared a secret with him.

The aged man often talked about his need to make a pilgrimage to Delhi or Calcutta in India on his knees—a journey which would involve many miles of rough and treacherous terrain. He believed this show of contrition would move the immortals to reward him. He even spoke of enjoying the hardship, imagining that by it he would achieve heaven. Naturally the missionary tried, albeit in vain, to talk him out of making such a journey. For one thing, the old man was old. The missionary tried to convince him that there was a real possibility he would be infected by some horrible disease. But most of all, he feared his aged friend would die without realizing his dream of achieving the immortals' reward; which, to the missionary may only be received as a gift when we believe in Jesus Christ.

The old man, determined to carry out his lifelong dream of completing the pilgrimage, removed from a Safe a large and flawless pearl wrapped in cloth, the likes of which the missionary had never seen before. Showing it to him with watery eyes, the old man announced his secret—it was from his son. In fact, it was the last pearl his son, who was also a diver, ever saw; for, while harvesting it from the ocean floor he stayed too long under water—he died giving his life for it.

You never told me you had a son!

I don't like to think about it; and talking about it makes me think about him. I can't stand the pain.

I'm so sorry to know you once had a son and suffered the pain of losing him.

The missionary kindly offered to purchase the pearl from his elderly friend, willing to pay him a generous sum of money. But his old friend would not hear of it.

"Sir," the old man replied, hardening himself to the idea of selling it, "There is no amount of money in the world that would pay for what this pearl is worth to me. I will never sell this; but I can give it to you as a gift."

"Not at all; I cannot just accept this without paying, it is too much, it is too easy; I must do something to earn it."

"Don't you understand?" The shocked elderly man replied, "This pearl is beyond price. My son gave his life for it. Its worth is in his lifeblood. But please take it as a token of our friendship and my deep affection for you."

Taking a moment to grasp the gravity of what he just experienced, the missionary realized this was the perfect opportunity to show the old man how he had been treating God's gift to him.

"Friend, don't you see? This is exactly what you have been saying to God. He is offering you eternal life as a free gift. It is so great and priceless nobody on earth can earn it. Like you, it cost God the life of His only Son. Doing a thousand pilgrimages would not be enough to pay for this priceless gift from God."

Suddenly the old man's eyes were opened. He saw for the first time that no amount of penance or good deeds could ever earn eternal life which was already paid for by the Lord Jesus Christ.

When it comes to getting right with God, we do not mind faith *and* good works, nor do we mind good deeds alone, but not faith alone. For some reason, human nature finds it troublesome having absolutely no part to play in their personal salvation. A hint from the Ephesians passage suggests that our egos (*so that none can boast*) may have something to do with our demand to contribute.

MISUNDERSTANDING SALVATION COMPLICATES BELIEF

Whenever I discuss this with people they instinctively respond, "You mean to tell me that people can say they believe in Jesus Christ and live anyway they choose and still go to heaven?" The idea of "faith alone" seems too weak and defenseless and is often misunderstood. But nowhere in the Bible will their line of reasoning find support. That common reaction reveals the widespread misunderstanding about the nature of God's salvation. When people exercise faith in Jesus Christ, something supernatural happens making it difficult to *live anyway they choose.*

The Holy Spirit's Role

The Holy Spirit takes up residence within each believer at the moment of faith (Ephesians 1:13; 2 Corinthians 1:22; Romans 8:9). Understand that this Spirit is Holy, i.e. He does not sit idly by and passively permit believers to *live anyway they want* without sensitizing their conscience, leading them to godliness, and teaching right from wrong (John 14:17, 26; John 16: 8, 13-14; Romans 8:14-16). Therefore, by virtue of the Holy Spirit within, true believers acquire an appetite for holiness, while at the same time there is an erosion of interest in things unholy. It is the Holy Spirit who empowers believers to love their enemies, forgive great injustices forced upon us, and restrain ourselves from following our natural impulses to sin. Without the Holy Spirit in us we are not true believers; we do not belong to God (Romans 8:9).

The Impure Cannot Produce Purity

Since we are imperfect beings there is no way we can offer anything that will satisfy a perfect and Holy God. The imperfect cannot generate perfection; the impure cannot produce purity. Anything we fabricate will fail to be good enough to gratify God. Hence, the well-known Scripture,

All our righteous deeds are like a filthy garment.
—Isaiah 64:6

101

Our very best aren't nearly good enough. (By the way, *filthy garment* here refers to a woman's used menstrual cloth). So the good works we do are not good enough. In fact, when offered to God along with our faith or in place of our faith to acquire salvation, good works are repulsive to Him. They are filthy.

This is not to say that good works are useless; on the contrary, God expects us to do kind deeds, but not as a requirement for salvation. We should be kind, loving, patient, and considerate to others but these acts of kindness can neither replace the sacrifice of Jesus Christ nor can they be added to it as an offering to God for our sins.

This was such a significant issue in the church of Galatia during the first century, that Paul wrote,

> If righteousness comes through the law, (*living an upstanding life by observing the code of the law*) then Christ died needlessly.
> —Galatians 2:21

In fact people's insistence upon it amounts to one of the greatest insults they can hurl at God. There is a real sense in which they are saying,

> God, your Son's sacrifice isn't quite good enough for me;
> let me offer You my good deeds either as a replacement
> for Him or in addition to Him.

When people place their faith in Jesus Christ, essentially they are transferring the trust and confidence they held in themselves or some other entity, over to Him. What God does next is absolutely unheard of. He gives Christ's righteousness to them (see Philippians 3:9). Since He alone satisfied God's holy standard, God will only accept Jesus' righteousness. God rightfully receives all the glory and man's ego is checked while it acknowledges God's mercy, and grace.

RIVAL BELIEF SYSTEMS COMPLICATE BELIEF

Attempts to believe in Jesus Christ may be daunting when some are unconvinced that He can meet their spiritual needs. Although there are numerous other barriers to faith in Jesus Christ, this bent toward good works remains their underlying obstacle. I do not pretend to know them all, but we will examine a few of the popular hurdles to faith in Jesus Christ.

Other gods

One hurdle is that some already believe in someone else who claims to be God or to whom deity has been ascribed. The globe is populated with large numbers of worshippers who were raised to believe in other gods. These are represented by various religions. They include Judaism, Islam, Confucianism, Hinduism, Sikhism, and Jehovah Witness to name only a few of the well-known ones. When people are nurtured to believe in a particular set of values, their loyalties are so cemented that it is difficult for them to even consider other possibilities. They often view them as rival gods and feel a sense of betrayal when faced with a choice to consider converting to a different belief system. This can complicate one's exercise of faith in the God of the Bible.

Atheism

Another reason it is difficult for some to believe in Jesus Christ to secure everlasting life constitutes a failure to believe in any god at all. Atheists are people who do not believe that

God exists. And since there is no God, according to them, Jesus Christ is a fictional character made up by Christians because they need an explanation for things they cannot explain. Or atheists may grant that Jesus is a historical figure but they may argue that men wrote the Bible to have something bigger than them in which to believe. Therefore, atheists find it difficult or even impossible to believe in Jesus Christ.

Humanism

Yet another reason some people do not believe in Jesus Christ for everlasting life is that they believe in themselves. They measure truth by themselves. Right, wrong, good, bad, and indifferent is approved by them. They are their own gods. They believe their own happiness and unhappiness results from their own doing. They make their own heaven and hell. Their destiny is in their own hands. Here again Jesus is not revered as the Son of God. They do not view Him as anything more than a mere man.

Christianity Appears Unattractive

A final reason people find it difficult to trust in Jesus Christ for everlasting life constitutes appeal. Many people who were raised in cultures with a predominant Christian influence, who also are not bound by any of the previous reasons simply do not find Jesus an attractive option. Jesus Christ is often presented as meek and mild, a person who allowed Himself to be killed on a wooden cross for others. And believers in Him are expected to live a boring, humble life, doing good for others. When window-shopping for a belief system with a comfortable fit and which looks good, Christ and Christianity aren't usually the chosen options.

They view Christianity as a life of church attendance and Bible study coupled with restrictions from the good life. This paradigm, incomplete at best and untrue at worst, is not attractive to many. As a result they would rather not place their trust in Him but in material things such as money which can buy them the things that excites them. These can make it complicated to believe in Jesus Christ for eternal life.

CHRISTIANS WITH BAD NAMES COMPLICATE BELIEF

Christians are not without blame for complicating the simplicity of faith for others to acquire eternal life. In fact, many may be responsible for driving away untold numbers of seekers by living hypocritical lives. Some preach an impossibly high standard of life and inevitably fail to honor the very message they propagate. Some are self-righteous, overly critical, judgmental, unkind, and unforgiving; thus, misrepresenting the *Christ* in Christians. And unfortunately, many people never read the Bible for themselves to examine its contents. If they did they would discover that Jesus Christ is grossly misrepresented by many who name the name of Christ. Jesus chided the religious leaders for this damaging fraud; and they endured His wrath since they had access to the truth. Gandhi, India's great liberator who espoused a Hindu set of beliefs, is famously quoted as saying,

> I like your Christ; I do not like your Christians. Your Christians are so unlike your Christ.
> —Mahatma Gandhi

One time a woman was caught in the act of adultery—a transgression committed by both men and women and punishable by stoning to death under Jewish law (see

Leviticus 20:10). The religious leaders (all men) brought only the woman to Jesus to seek His judgment. His reaction?

> He straightened up, and said to them, 'He who is without sin among you, let him be the first to throw a stone at her.
> —John 8:7

Upon hearing this, the self-appointed executioners one by one released their tight grasp from their carefully selected stones (the dust of self-righteousness still clinging to their fingers) and walked away with their heads hung in shame. In contrast, Jesus comforted the offending woman,

> Has anyone condemned you?
> No, master!
> Neither do I condemn you, go your way. From now on sin no more.
> —John 8:10-11

Many Christians never adopt this gentle and forgiving posture of Christ. Instead, they wield a holier-than-thou judgment gavel presenting an impossible and false portrait of the believer in Jesus Christ.

Another time Jesus scolded the religious leaders for being hypocrites,

> Woe to you, Scribes and Pharisees, hypocrites, because you travel about on sea and land to make one convert; and when he becomes one, you make him twice as much a son of hell as yourselves.
> —Matthew 23:15

Some Christian leaders invent unachievable standards and unrealistic rules not sanctioned by the Bible. Their followers, pressured to live up to those standards, fail; and as a consequence, adopt a life of hypocrisy. When in the presence of other Christians they pretend to keep those impossible, non-biblical, standards; but when they think no Christian eyes are upon them, they relax those expectations. This behavior confuses both believers and unbelievers alike.

In Romans 2:24, Paul referenced God's frustration with His people in Isaiah 52:5 when he said,

> The name of God is blasphemed among the Gentiles because of you.
>   —Isaiah 52:5; Romans 2:24

He was essentially stating that unbelievers are being foul-mouthed toward God because of how "people of God" sometimes live. Christians, it has been said, may be the only Bibles some unbelievers will ever read. So it is extremely important that believers not live hypocritical lives. This is why we read in David's most beloved Psalm that, as our shepherd, God leads believers in paths of righteousness. Why? "For His name's sake," His name (or reputation) is linked to His children and He will protect His name. Because, His reputation affects how outsiders view Him.

These confusing signals conspire to complicate the simplicity of faith in Jesus Christ.

BIBLICAL CHRISTIANITY UNIQUE AMONG RELIGIONS

Though there are many different religions, they all differ from Christianity at their core and they share one thing in common. They require a great deal of effort, performance, or good deeds to make it to their great reward, their nirvana, their paradise, their "heaven." Biblical Christianity is distinct from other religions in two fundamental ways:

1. It requires faith and only faith for one to inherit eternal life. No amount of human effort, regardless of how good, can substitute for the provision of Jesus Christ. He satisfied the God's justice with regard to sin's penalty by His holy sacrifice.

2. The other fundamental difference is that religion may be described as man's way to God; whereas, biblical Christianity is God's way to reach man. God, in the person of Jesus Christ came seeking man.

Religion does not possess these dynamics. As a result, faith's simplicity becomes complex. And since many people simply do not put their faith in Jesus, believing in the true and living God is made complicated.

CHAPTER 6 DISCUSSION QUESTIONS

1. How does our society view God's requirement for entrance into His kingdom?

2. What is the major disagreement with the idea that faith is all God requires for spiritual salvation?

3. What are some things which make it difficult to exercise faith in God?

4. How is biblical Christianity unique?

SECTION III

ENTERING THE HEIGHTS OF FAITH

Chapter 7

Faith—The Greatest Thrill

Such knowledge is too wonderful for me.
—Psalm 139:6.

Why didn't God refrain from introducing to mankind the "Tree of Knowledge of Good and Evil?" After writing that question, I literally covered my ears in anticipation of the resounding "YES!" I imagined readers will shout. Most people with whom I have discussed this question said that given the choice between knowing good & evil and remaining in innocence without knowing good & evil, they would choose to remain in innocence because the dark consequences of sin are just too great. Many believe that the world would be better off without that knowledge. We could do without it. It would have been worth not knowing good or evil to avoid the ravages of death, hate, murder, lying, stealing, and all the other by-products of sin. We don't know what we don't know.

On the surface, barring the "Tree of Knowledge of Good and Evil" from mankind appears to be an attractive option, especially when we are having a particularly bad day. But the fact remains that the placement of the tree in the center of Eden's orchard, by-and-large tested humanity's faithfulness.

Although our first parents plunged the entire world into sin and shattered the intimacy our forefather briefly enjoyed with God; the human race has been granted repentance and the people of faith have regained access to that intimacy with God.

Why then was it so important to have mankind's faith on trial? Why did God follow-through with a plan that allowed for sin? Didn't the All Knowing know the outcome beforehand? Of course He did! And if the reason He continued with His plan had nothing to do with Him learning the outcome (since He is omniscient and knows everything), then for whose benefit was this tree of testing permitted? The angels? Mankind? Whose?

May I suggest a line of thinking that may explain the reason for testing humanity's faithfulness to God?

GOD'S PLAN FOR A GREATER PRIZE

If we accept that God is perfect in every way, that is, He is without error, there is absolutely no flaw in Him, if this is true then we must also agree that unlike human beings with all our flaws, a perfect God cannot have a plan B. Selah. A plan B is essentially a contingency plan. It would mean that mistakes were possible, which amounts to imperfection. Plan B's exist as backups to the possible failings of plan A's. And since we are not willing to charge God with imperfection, we must be willing to look deeper. An inerrant God has only one plan; this magnificent world inclusive of all its problems is His plan A; it is all He needs. It has to be if He is indeed perfect. The current condition of the world did not result from an oversight by God. He saw this coming; better yet, He initiated this whole thing. When mankind disobeyed God, the

All Knowing One did not summon the Trinity to an emergency meeting to decipher what went wrong and figure out their next move. He was not taken by surprise. God was not nervously banging His anthropomorphic head against His jasper walls in despair, worrying that His perfect world was falling apart before His eyes. He was not ruffled. He was perfectly at peace. He made preparations in anticipation of humanity's fall into sin and corruption. And these preparations would lead John the Baptist to introduce Jesus as God's once-for-all remedy for sin. Pointing to Jesus, John announced:

> Behold, the Lamb of God who takes away the sin of the world.
>
> —John 1:29

As much as God hates sin and evil, He permitted them entrance into His perfect creation for a greater prize—our hearts. Our hearts are greater prizes because they represent that which we desire most. The heart has been defined as the seat of affections. The things we care about reside in our hearts. So God wants our hearts. He wants us to desire Him deeply of our own free will.

Joni Eareckson Tada, the paraplegic who became paralyzed in the prime of her youth seems to have understood why God allowed for sin when she said,

> Sometimes God allows what He hates to accomplish what He loves.

You'll agree that it often takes someone like Joni to appreciate what God is up to. Most of us are too busy with

113

our lives to stop and think beyond our immediate circumstances. But He cares much more than most realize. His interest in us goes beyond the surface. It goes straight to our hearts.

Intimacy with God

God is interested in intimacy with us; the very thing we desire most of all. The longing of every human heart is intimacy. We crave intimacy both with God and man. And since we were made in the image of God, this should come as no surprise to us. We are like Him in these ways.

Our great need for intimacy with God is evident by the countless number of worshipers blanketing the planet generation after generation. Comb through the following lines and see how a lover of God described the essence of his personal intimacy with the Son of God.

> I come to the garden alone
> While the dew is still on the roses
> And the voice I hear falling on my ear
> The Son of God discloses.

> *And He walks with me, and He talks with me,*
> *And He tells me I am His own;*
> *And the joy we share as we tarry there,*
> *None other has ever known.*

> He speaks, and the sound of His voice,
> Is so sweet the birds hush their singing,
> And the melody that He gave to me
> Within my heart is ringing.

I'd stay in the garden with Him
Though the night around me be falling,
But He bids me go; through the voice of woe
His voice to me is calling.

—Charles Austin Miles

Intimacy with Others

Our need for intimacy with our fellow man is even more obvious when we consider the extent to which we are willing to go in search of love and acceptance. The abundance of perfumes and colognes created to attract and entice the opposite sex; the poems written; the paintings and many forms of artwork depicting romance and love; the books written on the subject of love; the songs composed to express one's deepest feelings toward another points to considerable preoccupation with the need for intimacy. The lyrics to Diana Ross' and Lionel Richie's duet, Endless Love, expose the sentiments of many. Take a moment to revisit those engaging and all-encompassing words.

My love, there's only you in my life
The only thing that's right
My first love, you're every breath that I take
You're every step I make

—Diana Ross & Lionel Richie

INTIMACY FLOURISHES IN TRANSPARENCY

But true intimacy cannot be achieved in innocence. It flourishes in an environment where, along with its supporting cast (trust, loyalty, love, affirmation, volition, truth, and forgiveness) it is tested. The state of innocence Adam and Eve were in didn't generate the kind of intimacy we may enjoy with God. We needed to have our eyes wide open to know what we're getting ourselves into. The "Tree of Knowledge of Good and Evil" provided that environment. Intimacy is produced in an environment of informed faith.

It has always been considered bullying to prey upon the innocent. Taking advantage of people who are not fully aware of what they are getting into is at best inconsiderate, and at worst, downright wicked. Intimacy involves knowingly and voluntarily sharing one's heart with another. There must be volition, there has to be voluntary choice. By affording us the power of choice, God's plan allowed for the highest form of intimacy possible between God and man (Exodus 25:8; John 17:24; 1 John 3:2). He wants to share Himself with us and He wants us to want to share ourselves with Him. To leave us in innocence without giving us the option to choose Him would be dictatorial and would restrict us to a robotic existence. Such an existence would make it possible to follow directives, but impossible to participate in a mutually vulnerable and trusting relationship—one wherein we can plumb the depths of intimacy. As Creator, He could have exercised that sterile option but God had higher ideals for us.

BASKING IN GOD'S GLORY

Since He Himself is the highest ideal, He invites us to bask in His glory. We get to share in His amazing grace. We are afforded a taste of His magnificence. The creature is elevated to enter into the Creator's splendor. When we do, we find the only fitting response is that of gratitude, awe and wonder in worshipful adoration of Him.

Some of you may remember the meaningful little song we learned as children. Its lines seem to capture nature's fitting response to her benevolent Creator:

> The birds upon the tree tops sing their song;
> The angels chant their chorus all day long;
> The flowers in the garden blend their hue,
> So why shouldn't I, why shouldn't you praise Him too?
> —Author Unknown

England's Thomas Ken may have been thinking along similar lines or of Psalm 103 when he penned the Doxology. In it we, along with all other beings, both heavenly and earthly, are summoned to worship the Almighty.

> Praise God from whom all blessings flow
> Praise Him all creatures here below
> Praise Him above ye heavenly hosts
> Praise Father, Son, and Holy Ghost
> —Thomas Ken

These songs of worship show all God's creatures paying homage to Him, shouldn't we do likewise? He has proven Himself generous, kind, caring and glorious. It is the appropriate thing to do. But we must choose Him. When we do, we get to bask in His glory; we get to experience the greatest heights of elation, joy, fulfillment, and contentment knowable only to those who worship God uninhibited.

THE PLACE OF SUFFERING

But this could not happen in innocence. It required full disclosure from God even about the knowledge of evil.

Because, in God's plan sin and evil have a role to play. He uses everything for His glory. The by-products of sin contribute to God's glory much like the black cloth used as background by jewelers provides the contrast that heightens the diamond's glory.

It is exposure to suffering, disappointment, pain, loss, hunger, cruelty, insults and all manner of abuse we both perpetrate and endure that creates the longing for rest, peace, goodness, love, acceptance, and all that is wholesome. No one would be able to appreciate good health when all they ever knew was perfect health. Our minds and senses would have nothing to compare to a beautiful, bright, and sunny day had we never encountered the dread of a cold, wet, dark and dreary day. Our hearts and minds are more receptive when great pain is replaced by great ease; whereas, a life of ease devoid of disappointments tends to produce shallowness and banality.

Internationally respected author and Christian apologist, Ravi Zacharias, has been known to advance the notion that meaninglessness does not come from being weary of pain; it comes from being weary of pleasure. This is a proven principle. The things we deem most precious don't usually come easy; they are often birthed out of great struggle. For a diamond to be made, it undergoes intense and sustained pressure which removes all softer elements. Refined gold is likewise birthed through great degrees of intense heat. To get to a beautiful rose, one must contend with the thorns. It is a universal principle. Innocence does not elevate us to the highest heights; we need volition, we need personal choice. Ignorance isn't always bliss; ignorance may be blight.

The Deeper the Pain; The Greater the Rejoicing

In addition to being compassionate, kind, gracious and going around doing good deeds, Jesus is also well reputed for His mastery of the art of storytelling. On one occasion, He brought to light this principle of glory through gloom.

During His brief visit to our planet, He accepted an invitation to dine at the home of a Pharisee (Jewish religious scholar and leader). While reclining at the table, a woman who had gained notoriety for being a sinner (in this case probably a prostitute) followed Him into the house, and broke down in tears at His feet. Now it was customary in that culture to provide a jar of water and a towel for guests to have their feet washed from the dust so plenteous in that region. But none was provided Jesus when He entered Simon's house. Using her tears for water, this deeply hurt and dejected woman washed Jesus' dusty feet. She then used her hair as a towel to dry them off.

When Simon the Pharisee saw this, he concluded that Jesus could not possibly have any favorable connection to God. He reasoned within himself that a prophet would know what sort of woman was touching Him. The plot thickened. The narrator explained that at this point Jesus addressed the private thoughts Simon had been entertaining to comfort himself. [Isn't that just typical? When a better man is in our presence, we sometimes look for a flaw in him so we can elevate ourselves above him.]

The honored guest told the Pharisee a story exposing his thoughts. In classic non-confrontational style, Jesus told Simon about a financier who had two debtors: One owed five hundred denarii (A denarius was a roman denomination of money worth a day's wage), and the other fifty. When these were unable to pay their debts, the moneylender forgave them both. At this point in the narrative, I imagine Jesus looking straight into the eyes of His host, Simon, when He posed the next question,

> Which of them therefore will love him more?
>
> —Luke 7:42

By now the Pharisee, realizing his holier-than-thou reasoning had been exposed, clears his throat, swallows nervously and ekes out an answer,

> I suppose the one he forgave more.
>
> —Luke 7:43

"Right!" Jesus said, "You've judged correctly."

This story illustrates common experiences faced by billions of people every day: The deeper the pain, the greater the rejoicing. There is a direct relationship between the scale of violation and the magnitude of joy experienced when the violation is forgiven. The one who is forgiven most is the one who appreciates it most and therefore loves most.

> He who has stood before his God, convicted and condemned, with the rope about his neck, is the man to weep for joy when he is pardoned, to hate the evil which has been forgiven him, and to live to the honour of the Redeemer by whose blood he has been cleansed.
>
> —Charles Spurgeon

That woman, because of her burdened heart, was compelled to follow Jesus into Simon's house uninvited—so great was her need for forgiveness. The Pharisees, who were notorious legalists, held everyone to a strict observance of Jewish laws containing 613 do's and don'ts. They were self-righteous and thought of themselves as better than everyone else. Since in their hearts and minds they never did anything wrong, they never had anything to rejoice about. There was nothing to triumph over.

We Must be Lost Before We Can be Found

At one time, Jesus spoke out against that self-righteous pharisaic trait. He said,

> I did not come to call the righteous (*self-righteous people like the Pharisees*); but sinners to repentance.
> —Matthew 9:13

People must be lost before they can be found; they have to be spiritually bankrupted before they can be saved. How do you lead an alcoholic to sobriety when he is convinced that he is not drunk? Nothing shackles Christ's rescuing hands quite like self-righteousness. He can do absolutely nothing for us until we acknowledge our need. God's plan A, His perfect and solitary plan, necessitated a downside.

Admittedly, this is not always easy to understand largely because of the opposing position sin occupies against the holy nature of God. Of all the Almighty's many attributes, holiness is central to His character. Each of His other attributes emanate from His holiness. Therefore, there must be a greater purpose for sin's inclusion into His plan for humankind. And the greatest purpose God has revealed to us in His Word is His glory.

FAITH BEFORE GLORY

Not only was it necessary for us to exercise volition in choice; but, our choice of Him reveals our faith in Him and is required before we can bask in His glory.

At the tomb of Lazarus the brother of Mary and Martha friends of Jesus, the Master-Teacher about to show His power, turned to His disciples and reminded them,

> Did I not say to you that if you would believe, you would see the glory of God?
>
> —John 11:40

What a statement! What a profound spiritual principle to stop and make sure they understood. The order here is important; believe first and then the glory will be revealed. We tend to have the order reversed. We would much rather see the glory first, and then we think we will believe. I say, think, because it is a fallacy.

I have heard many skeptics say, "If God is real why doesn't He come down here and prove it? Then I will believe Him." My response is always the same, "He did!" And this sometimes stuns them because they weren't expecting that response. Two thousand years ago He arrived in our backyard to the sound of John the Baptist and angels announcing His arrival and identifying Him as the Son of God. He had no human father, He backed up His own claims to deity by living a sinless life, performed miracles, and finally died and defied death three days later, all according to His and other prophets' predictions. So the order is right. First we must believe and then we will see the glory.

Maybe Augustine understood this principle when he penned the words,

> Faith is to believe what we do not see; and the reward of this faith is to see what we believe.
>
> —St. Augustine

Clearly, he got the order right. Of course, we are talking about an informed belief; not a blind faith.

On another occasion, Jesus was about to revive a woman who had died. The usual suspects—the Pharisees and Scribes—laughed Him to scorn when He announced to them that, as far as He was concerned, she was merely asleep. At their behavior, Jesus asked them to leave the room. When they left, Jesus restored the life of the woman. Because of their unbelief, they forfeited the privilege to witness a miracle. They missed a glorious opportunity.

When I was young and first read this, I couldn't understand why Jesus insisted that they leave the room simply because they did not believe. One possible reason is that when people make up their minds that a certain thing cannot be done, even if they see that thing being done they refuse to acknowledge the source responsible for getting it done. Regardless of what anybody says they will find some other explanation to satisfy their preconceived disbelief. So if Jesus allowed them to stay and witness the miracle, they would find some way to minimize the power of God in raising her from the dead.

I am reminded of the case a psychiatrist once told about. One of his patients thought himself to be dead. Somehow he convinced himself that he was a living corpse. No one could convince him he was alive. After offering him every reasonable explanation that he couldn't be dead, the psychiatrist came up with a plan. He would prove to his patient that dead people don't bleed. So he gave him several books to read and had him return at an appointed time to discuss the reading. The patient read the books and was prompt at their scheduled appointment.

The psychiatrist started off, "What did you find in your reading?"

"Medical evidence proves that dead men don't bleed," he answered.

"So if a person bleeds we know they are not dead, right?" confirmed the psychiatrist.

"Absolutely!" The patient said.

This was the moment the psychiatrist was hoping for. He took a pin and pricked the patient's finger causing a bubble of blood to form on the tip.

The patient looked at his finger in shock and said, "Oh my goodness, dead people do bleed after all."

Nothing could change his stubborn unbelief. It is with that kind of thinking Jesus is deemed a failure before He has begun. Now, God will not compromise His glory. It is fitting that God is credited when He changes things. I have seen this happen over and over again. The human will can be extremely stubborn. Sometimes it is face-saving pride that keeps the stubborn from letting go of an idea being held on to for a long time.

I have often wondered if one of the reasons God made some things humanly impossible before He stepped in and performed a miracle was to make it clear that no one else but He alone could have performed such a feat and therefore He alone must be credited for the performance. For instance, it is clear that, in Scripture, when God was about to do something really big especially in regard to our spiritual salvation, He first made the conditions impossible then He made it possible only through His power. He did this on several occasions.

Ship on a Hill

One occasion concerns the flood of Noah's day. By chapter six of the beginning book in the Bible, Genesis, we read that God was so disgusted with man's constant stream of evil on the earth that He decided to wipe out everyone except the one righteous person, Noah, and his family. As you may recall, the ancient ark was built on a mountain. How was Noah to get it down to the ocean? That whole ordeal would have been impossible if he didn't first believe God and then build the ark according to His specifications, far away from the ocean, and in the face of hecklers laughing him to scorn (not unlike the men in Peter's house).

Barren and Old

Another instance had to do with God's long-term plan for spiritual salvation whereby Jesus Christ would eventually be born and pay for the sins of the world with His life. Jesus' ancestral lineage through Abraham, Isaac, Jacob, David, and Mary required God's supernatural intervention. So when God was about to create the nation of Israel through Abraham, his wife Sarah was found to be barren. She was unable to have children. To make matters worse, she was old and past childbearing age. Is that impossible enough? But God promised that through Abraham and His wife Sarah, he was going to have an heir through whom the messiah would come. In the historic record we read that:

> Abraham believed God and God reckoned it to him as righteousness.
>
> —Genesis 15:6

We are familiar with the rest of the story. Sarah bore Abraham a son, Isaac. God wanted Abraham to be so sure about His promise that he entered into an unconditional contract with Him in which He alone signed the contract.

In Old Testament days when two parties entered into a covenant, they split a calf in two and together they passed between the pieces to ratify (sign) the covenant/contract (see Jeremiah 18:34). But God did it differently with Abraham, He had him array the calf in its parts and then caused him to fall into a trance so that he could be aware of what was happening but unable to walk between the split parts. See Genesis 15 for the whole fascinating narrative. In verses 17 and 18 we read,

> And it came about when the sun had set, that it was very dark, and behold, there appeared a smoking oven and a flaming torch which passed between these pieces. On that day the LORD made a covenant with Abram.
>
> —Genesis 15:17-18

God went to extraordinary lengths to ensure that Abraham did not walk between those parts with Him. Because He alone was going to do this impossible thing, He alone signed the contract. And He also wanted Abraham to rest assured that He can be trusted to pull off the impossible. Who else may be credited when the promise is fulfilled but God?

Barren and Virgin

Although there are other examples of God making things impossible before He showed up to intervene, we will look at just one more. Consider the plight of both Elizabeth, the mother of John the Baptist, and Mary the mother of Jesus. Elizabeth was also barren for many years before giving birth to John (Luke 1:5-25). This was important because God was going to use John to introduce Jesus the Son of God to the world.

But the case of Mary is even more amazing. Recall that Mary was a teenage virgin who never knew a man; yet, the Bible tells us that the Holy Spirit overshadowed her and she was found to be with child (Luke 1:26-38). That child was Jesus Christ whom John introduced as the Lamb of God who takes away the sin of the world. Who else could possibly be credited with that but God?

So it is important that when God has provided us with ample reasons to believe in Him, we place our faith in Him without asking Him to keep proving Himself over and over again. Will He not point us to the evidence He already provided? He is God and not a man that we could play with Him. That behavior is known as hardening your hearts and testing God. When we fail to take God at His Word, especially after demonstrating His trustworthiness, we are effectively discrediting His character. We are treating Him as a liar and deceiver. Believe first—not blindly of course—and then we will see His power and glory.

GOD'S GLORY IS ULTIMATE

The glory of God appears to be His ultimate goal for all creation. Contrary to popular teaching, the Christian's primary occupation is not evangelism (winning converts to Christ). As important as evangelism is, it is only a means to a higher good—the glory of God! Glorifying God in worship supersedes anything we can ever do. That's ultimate! Evangelism exists because there is a deficiency in worship, a deficiency in glorifying God. Too many people are directing their praise and worship to the wrong recipient; therefore, evangelism is needed to persuade people that although their intentions may be honorable, the God of the Bible is their Creator, the true and living God to whom their adoration and gratitude ought to be directed.

Jesus left no doubt about this in John 4 when He corrected the view of a Samaritan woman. The ancient record reveals that she came to draw water out of Jacob's well under the sweltering midday heat. As a conversation between the pair developed, she talked about her ancestors' worship practices taking place in a certain mountain. Jesus, concerned about the misdirection of her worship, sought to redirect her to the true and living God. The engaging exchange rapidly led to a statement which encapsulates the very purpose for His mission to our planet:

> Jesus said to her, Woman, believe Me, an hour is coming when neither in this mountain nor in Jerusalem will you worship the Father. You worship what you do not know; we worship what we know, for salvation is from the Jews. But an hour is coming, and now is, when the true worshipers will worship the Father in spirit and truth; for such people the *Father seeks to be His worshipers*. God is spirit, and those who worship Him must worship in spirit and truth.
>
> —John 4:21-23

Notice the words in italics—God is seeking worshipers. Evangelism is a means to an end—worship. It is the big deal with God and the very purpose for our existence (Isaiah 43:7). It is the big dance. The glory of God is where the action is. It is the reason we read that God is a jealous God—He does not entertain rivals. Nothing and no one is comparable with Him. To enter into His glory we must exercise faith first.

IDOLS OF THE HEART THREATEN INTIMACY

These truths however, do not discourage humans from erecting the millions of gods we craft in our hearts everyday. Apart from the physical idols etched on wood, stone, and metals by worshipers in every corner of the globe, people carve out idols-of-the-heart (Ezekiel 14:3) which occupy that position reserved only for our Creator. They attempt to fill that spot in their hearts belonging to God. The obvious and well-known culprits include money, people, and time.

Money buys a life of ease and is a favorite idol of the masses. A life focused on ease makes it easy to forget God.

When people become idols they invade the space God alone should occupy in our hearts. They come in all forms—spouses, children, friends, and family.

Excessive time devoted to the things which advance our own interests to bring only personal gratification trumps the time we may spend advancing God's program.

The tricky thing is all of the idols mentioned are legitimate gifts from God. But these legitimate gifts become illegitimate gods (idols), and are therefore, perversions when they pull off a spiritual coup d'état and usurp God's place in our hearts. That supreme place belongs to the Supreme One.

When that sacred place is invaded by rivals, God's glory is compromised in our hearts. As a result, our lives veer off the path to actualizing our full potential of being all that we were designed to be. So instead of growing more intimate with the God of love, we distance ourselves by erecting barriers to nearness with Him.

It is only in spiritual closeness to Him that we get glimpses of His glory. Our unyielding faith and loyalty to Him unleashes the floodgates of blessing. When our agendas are aligned with His, we are brought into His confidence and made privy to some of His secrets (see Psalm 25:14; 91:1). And during moments of our faith's testing we discover the futility of our idols. Testing our faith causes us to refocus upon God's ultimate sovereignty.

WORSHIP BLOWS OUR CIRCUITS

There is a shared benefit when God is worshiped and glorified. On the one hand, God is acknowledged, praised, worshiped, adored, loved, awed, and glorified, as is fitting— He is God and fully deserves the adulation of His creatures. On the other hand, we enter into the highest possible experience the human can know. The worship and glorification of God is a privilege that "blows all our circuits."

Even the angels of God who inhabit His presence every moment have not been granted the sobering heights of ecstasy humans can reach. Like us, some (1/3) in the angelic order committed treason against their Maker; unlike us however, those who did were not permitted repentance. Therefore they cannot enter into the realms of awareness humans, who have been granted repentance, can. It is totally foreign to them. In fact, the apostle Peter relates that the angels possess strong curiosity about human salvation (I Peter 1:12). They literally strain their necks trying to get a glimpse and understanding of human salvation.

Years ago I came across the popular newspaper cartoon, Family Circus. As I recall, the little boy is seen joyfully strolling along with a gigantic smile splashed across his face. Underneath, the hilarious caption stated, "I'm so happy, if I had a tail, I would wag it." That's the picture Peter paints. Angels' wings would twitch and flutter with excitement at the prospect. But they can neither fully understand nor appreciate forgiveness and its ensuing joys.

Here is how Johnson Oatman Jr., (1856-1922) expressed his overwhelming awe and wonder at this truth over a century ago:

There is singing up in Heaven
such as we have never known,
Where the *angels* sing the praises
of the Lamb upon the throne,
Their sweet harps are ever tuneful,
and their voices always clear,
O that we might be more like them
while we serve the Master here!

Holy, holy, is what the angels sing,
And I expect to help them
make the courts of heaven ring;
But when I sing redemption's story,
they will fold their wings,
For angels never felt the joys
that our salvation brings.

But I hear another anthem,
blending voices clear and strong,
"Unto Him Who hath redeemed us
and hath bought us," is the song;
We have come through tribulation
to this land so fair and bright,
In the fountain freely flowing
He hath made our garments white.

Then the *angels* stand and listen,
for they cannot join the song,
Like the sound of many waters,
by that happy, blood washed throng,
For they sing about great trials,
battles fought and vict'ries won,
And they praise their great Redeemer,
who hath said to them, "Well done."

So, although I'm not an *angel*,
yet I know that over there
I will join a blessèd chorus
that the *angels* cannot share;
I will sing about my Savior,
who upon dark Calvary
Freely pardoned my transgressions,
died to set a sinner free
—Johnson Oatman Jr.

He who has been forgiven most glorifies most. As the fourth stanza says, the angels stand and listen because they cannot participate in humans' redemption song. They remain in innocence and cannot appreciate forgiveness.

Israel's beloved king David, dubbed by God, "A man after My own heart," poured forth his awe and wonder of God in Psalm 8:

O Lord, our Lord,
How majestic is your name in all the earth!
You have set your glory above the heavens.

When I consider your heavens, the work of your fingers,
the moon and the stars, which You have set in place,
What is man that You are mindful of him,
the son of man that You care for him?

You made him a little lower than the heavenly beings
and crowned him with glory and honor.
You made him ruler over the works of Your hands;
You put everything under his feet:
All flocks and herds, and the beasts of the field,
the birds of the air, and the fish of the sea,
All that swim the paths of the sea.

O Lord, our Lord,
How majestic is your name in all the earth!

Glorifying God is not a drag; it is joyous and filled with wonder. It leaves us elated and ecstatic. When the Creator conceived of us and designed us, He wired us with great capacity to be happiest when found in the act of uninhibited worship and glorification of God. We are programmed for worship.

When we do not glorify Him, we seek thrills and excitement to satisfy a gaping need that refuses go away. As a thoughtful designer, it is God who wrote our genetic code with capabilities of exceeding the highest heights in glory. It stands to reason therefore, that He knows best how to "blow our circuits" with excitement.

GOD DOES NOT PRODUCE BORING CHRISTIANS

He Designed Us for Excitement

Do these phrases have a familiar ring? That was awesome! What a rush! What a thrill! These expressions of excitement usually follow events "booby-trapped" with risks.

Some teenagers, for instance, may be found driving around corners at speeds exceeding 80 mph in search of a buzz (I confess, I was guilty of this activity). Some thrill-seekers bungee-jump off cliffs in death-defying stunts, with only a rope tied around their ankles (I am happy to confess, I have never had any ambition for this). Some, even at an advanced age, seeking to induce a jolt of adrenaline-rush through their veins, opt to leap out of aircrafts miles above ground.

It appears that the risks grow greater each summer when amusement parks reopen boasting bigger and more convoluted, death-defying rides. And some, unfortunately, plunge to their deaths having been overcome by those risks. What exactly are people seeking?

It may be little surprise to learn that they are in active pursuit of satisfying a supernatural craving deep within the heart—a craving God placed in humanity's spiritual DNA. This craving may leave us frustrated if left unsatisfied. But when the adrenalin rushes from those thrill-seeking risks subside, we tend to pursue an even greater risk-laden adventure dangling (like the proverbial carrot) an even greater promise of fulfillment; for, the previous thrill level has lost its appeal. The experience leaves many, like dogs, chasing their proverbial tails.

Disappointment with Stolen Pleasure

I remember listening to a radio program and hearing the speaker relate a story he referred to as, "The Adulterous Woman," who was married to a wealthy businessman. If I recall correctly, the woman had a private fantasy of being more liberal than her husband usually was in the bedroom. However, she loved her husband and never wanted to hurt him in any way.

On one occasion, she accompanied her husband on an out-of-town business trip. His plan was to attend the required meetings and then spend the rest of the time together with his wife. But his wife's fantasy began to consume her and she sought opportunity in the strange city to explore her dreams without anyone ever finding out. While her husband attended his conferences, she spent all day consumed with the notion of finally fulfilling her wildest imaginations. Their last night there, her husband arrived home exhausted and fell asleep. 'It would be now or never,' she thought. While her husband was asleep she slipped out into the night, went and indulged her craving and returned to find him still sound asleep on the bed. In the stillness of the night, her husband was awakened by loud sobbing noises. Turning to his wife, he asked her what upset her so terribly. Her reply to him was informative. In the most painful and disappointing tone she said,

Nothing! Absolutely nothing!

The thrill she thought she so greatly needed left her with a haunting feeling of disappointment. In her own words, "nothing" happened. She remained unsatisfied and grew increasingly frustrated. If truth be told, more pain happened.

Yet, the satisfaction we receive when we enter into worship and glorification of God doesn't leave us disappointed. It doesn't increase our need for higher levels of risk. We don't have to keep reaching for some elusive promise of ecstasy. On the contrary, glorifying God leaves us satisfied, contented, affirmed, at rest, and peaceful. It gives us a sense of satisfaction deeply known in our innermost beings. This phenomenon stands in stark contrast with those who attach boredom to being a person of faith.

Excitement in Variety of Beauty

God cannot be charged with boredom. To charge God with boredom is comparable to accusing the designer of a well-made car of boredom because you don't know how to drive. Far from it! God Himself hates boredom.

Just look around! Consider what He has done with nature. Take a moment to observe the blue skies, white clouds, the soft and distant moon, the twinkling stars, the vast oceans, the recycling seasons, the tropical islands, the arctic lands, the generations and variety of fishes, the various land and sky animals, and the list is endless. Consider the variety in size, function, purposes, color, texture, form, and habitat of the elements, trees, animals, and people.

I recall vividly, the first time I noticed an Asian youth. As a toddler filled with awe and wonder at the variety of people God had created. I remember my jaw falling open and my eyes growing wide in curious astonishment at this cute and very different looking little person. We are all so similar and yet very different: Some tall, others short, many of average height, the spectrum of color accounting for every shade imaginable.

The variety evident in an individual's ability is nothing short of staggering. Some people are gifted scientists; others include great athletes, writers, artists, administrators, politicians, leaders, orators, craftsmen, jewelers, designers, and the list is limited only by our imagination. This colorful variety in ability has the habit of leaving us awe-struck when we experience our athletes and artists in their element. No! God is not boring, at all.

Excitement from Our Talents

David Beckham, for instance, had been made famous for his ability to kick a soccer ball. He occupied the right midfield position on the field of play and it was his job to get crosses in to the forwards for them to score goals. No one in the world is quite as good as he was in staving off defenders and picking out his attacking teammate, who was running into scoring position with two or three top notch, highly trained defenders breathing down his neck. Beckham's greatness was amplified when he was able to bend the ball around these defenders and place it exactly on the head, chest, thigh, or feet of his striking teammate, say Dwight Yorke, to bury the item in the back of the net. More often than not he scored goals. No! Absolutely not! God is not at all boring. Hence the popular movie with the title, *Bend It Like Beckham*.

One time Michael Jordan collected the ball from a teammate among a flurry of slashing and swiping, sweaty hands and went into "Jordan-esk" mode. Complete with tongue flapping in the wind, he rocketed up to the basket and was about to slam one home when he noticed a defender about to attempt a block-shot. What does he do? He instinctively carves out an eternity of time in his domain, the air, and sneaks the ball around to the side of the basket for one of the most memorable displays forever etched in every sports enthusiast's memory. All this, while on his way back down to earth from rarefied air.

When we observe a recording artist play her instrument as if she is giving her soul to the moment with eyes closed, voice relaxed and effortlessly powerful, overcome with emotion we all vicariously feel we can do as she is doing.

If you ever heard Whitney Houston, Amy Grant, Michael McDonald, or Larnelle Harris paint a picture and tell a story in song, you will know that God is not boring.

I used to wonder whether my mother was somehow crossed with a species of octopus. 'There is no other explanation,' I thought, 'for her being able to accomplish the number of things she accomplished all at once without incurring a major accident.' As I grew older, I have since learned that women tend to multitask more or better than men; although, some men multitask very well and some women can't chew gum and walk.

If that notion (that God is boring) is popular anywhere, maybe Christians and people of faith must take responsibility for misrepresenting the most creative and exciting being in the universe—God.

Excitement in Other Human Experiences

The function of the palate is to provide pleasure and enjoyment of the many varieties of delicacies available to us.

We didn't need it to be able to eat and sustain life. That detail in our design couldn't derive from a boring God.

Similarly with procreation, God didn't have to make this special, marital experience an enjoyable and pleasurable one for humans to be fruitful and multiply. But that is just like God. He is far from boring; He wants us to discover new levels of intimacy with each other.

God intended us to work. This is clear from the Genesis account even before the fall. But here again He made the exercise enjoyable by granting each person special ability to perform their jobs with a great measure of satisfaction. It is He who endowed the likes of Michael Angelo, Mozart, Stephen Spielberg, Amy Carmichael, Pele, and Michael Jordan with their creative skills to "wow" the world and in the process evoke in us that special quality which lead us to glorify God.

More often than not, I find myself understanding the sentiments of Gandhi who expressed love for Christ but disdain for some Christians who would have us believe that a boring life pleases God. Nothing could be further from the truth. This insults our Creator. God exceeds our imagination. We learn in the New Testament from the apostle Paul that human eyes have not even seen, nor have our ears heard, neither has it entered our wildest imaginations the things God has prepared for those who love Him. Wow! What is God up to next?

RISK IS NATURAL TO FAITH AND ADVENTURE

The risk we find so prevalent among thrill-seekers is not coincidental. That mystique for which a person is willing to brave the odds is not unique to the nature of risk; it is also natural to the habitat of faith. The life of faith is meant to be an adventure with God; not as so many make it, a contest to decide who could live the most somber, uninteresting existence. We were not made for the grey, careful, banal and dull existence; although, these are necessary and important experiences which brighten the glory of appreciative awe and wonder. We were designed to explore the wonders of God. And these wonders are adventurous and involve risk.

I remember visiting a friend's home and noticing hung upon his living-room wall a beautiful artwork depicting ships docked at the harbor. What gave me pause and food for thought was the caption written just beneath the painting. "Ships are beautiful to look at in the harbor," the first line seemed to whisper, "But that is not what ships are made for," the second line seemed to shout. Ships were made to be out in the ocean braving the rough waves beating against their bows. Like ships, God did not create us just to be spectacles, but to get out into His world and engage.

Faith and trust inherently involve risk. If we were to cut into the fabric of faith, it would bleed risk. We believe and follow God based on an informed risk; some call it a calculated risk. Because of what is known and knowable about God, we risk the unknown on His omnipotent ability to produce and deliver.

One of the unknowns often proves to be His timing. The patriarch Abraham grew impatient with God's timing as he advanced in age even though he believed God would follow-through with His promise to unlock Sarah's barren womb and have them cuddle a son of their own. The record revealed that Sarah was 90 years young and Abraham celebrated his centennial year when their son Isaac finally arrived. What an adventure that must have been?

This appears to be one of God's usual modus operandi; He adds that suspense and drama associated with adventure. Just when it appears He has forgotten us and we are about to give up, He arrives ready to perform, just as He promised.

GOD'S RISKY INVESTMENT IN HUMANS

God does not need to exercise faith since He is all-knowing; even though, He does things which appear to be risky even to Him. It may be said that God took risks on us.

He risked His reputation when permitting humans partnership in coauthoring His inerrant Word. To this day the uninformed still claim that men wrote the Bible despite the Bible's clear declaration of dual-authorship and being God-breathed.

The Fearless One risked both His good name and the quantity of converts when He again partnered with believers to accomplish the important work of making disciples and seeking worshipers (Matthew 28:18-20; 2 Corinthians 5:19). Interestingly, He didn't need us to partner with Him in order to accomplish this, but because He is relational and intimate with us, He included us in this thrilling venture.

He has taken the risk of a plan that includes sin. Sin ruined much but it cannot touch everything. God's forgiveness and grace is greater than sin's blows.

God has taken the risk of having His Son (of whom one of His titles is the Prince of Life) experience death along with bearing the weight of the world's accumulated trans-generational sins. Imagine, if you can, all of your or someone's jealousy, envy, hatred, cynicism, if you murdered (including abortions), lies, robberies, adulteries, disrespect for parents and the list is long. Multiply that by seven billion people. That count is only in this generation. Now place all of those sins and the sins of everyone throughout all generations from the beginning of time in one man's body. Did I mention that this one man never ever sinned once in His life? This unfathomable number of the ugliest substance foreign to Christ invaded His Holy body when they were dumped upon Him at Calvary. What if His tomb never opened? What a risk!

God is a father and leader who led by example. He has taken upon Himself the bigger risk by asking us to trust Him. Many don't. He could have had us all like robots, worshiping without having chosen Him. Instead, He gave us choice and many worshippers chose to worship false gods. As a result, His name and glory is treated with contempt every day.

TESTED FAITH REVEALS OUR PROXIMITY TO GOD

The trial of man's faith in Eden was necessary to give us the opportunity to choose God above all else. It is also necessary on an ongoing basis as it provides the greatest commentary about where we are in our relationship with God; it shines an unmistakable spotlight upon the degree of intimacy we share with Him. There is a sense in which the trial of our faith tells us how we're doing with God.

Everything of value is assessed by the consumer before committing to payment. When, for instance, I was in the market to sell my house, I contacted a real estate agent who possessed expertise in purchasing and marketing residential property. After our initial conversation, the agent counseled me to have the property appraised so that we may know the house's market-value at that time. Like my house, our faith is appraised for its value, its strength, its authenticity.

Also, when our faith is tested it strips away all our excuses and strains out all the defilements in our character. It exposes the arrogance we attempt to cover up. And it ultimately leads us to our desperate need for intimacy with God. It allows us to adjust to Him; we see the obvious need to realign ourselves to Him. When we emerge triumphant from the rigors of a trial, we either learn or confirm how strong we are (with God's help) in that particular area of our lives, at that particular time in our lives. The converse is also true. When we fail a test we learn or confirm our suspicions that we still have work to do in that particular area of our lives.

Independence from our creator is tantamount to spiritual suicide; whereas, dependence upon Him feeds spiritual life. Our faith in Him is that spiritual lifeline. Just as a branch is sustained as long as it stays attached to the tree; so we are spiritually healthy as long as we, by faith, stay attached to God.

The value God places on us is so high that our faith must be tested; the intimacy so precious that the trial of our faith is proven invaluable. (By the way, we do well to keep in mind that God knows the outcome of the test beforehand. God does not test us so *He* might discover something about us; He tests us that *we* might find out where we are in relation to trusting Him.) Hudson Taylor, missionary to China, understood this, using the word pressure for test, he said:

> It really doesn't matter *how great* the pressure is; it only matters *where* the pressure lies. See that it doesn't come between you and the Lord. The greater the pressure the closer it presses you to His breast.

The comparison is often made with the process of producing the precious metal, gold. As heat is needed to refine gold by removing all dross and impurities from the metal; similarly, the heat of trials removes excuses, and exposes the genuineness of our loyalty to God.

> The crucible is for refining silver and the furnace is for gold, but the Lord tests hearts.
>
> —Proverbs 17:3

One of Jesus' closest disciples, Peter, who emerged as the group's spokesperson attempted to comfort the Christians dispersed throughout Asia Minor, which is in the region of modern-day Turkey. These early Christian disciples were scattered because of the threat of persecution in Jerusalem. How do you comfort a persecuted people fleeing for their lives because of their beliefs? Peter showed them how the trial of their faith was so valuable that it surpassed the riches of temporal and material comforts and resulted in praise, glory, and honor (see 1 Peter 1:7).

Our faith's trial reveals our loyalty to the greatest of all:

The greatest person (*God*)

The greatest giver (*the giver of life*);

The greatest lover (*the one who loved and gave Himself for us*);

The greatest judge (*the one who judges righteously*);

The greatest creditor (*He's willing to forgive us of our greatest debt [our sin leading to eternity in hell]*) and,

The most faithful of all (*the one who will never leave us nor forsake us*).

What a thrill with the Greatest in the universe—God.

֍

CHAPTER 7 DISCUSSION QUESTIONS

1. How does God's plan for intimacy explain the placement of the *Tree of Knowledge of Good and Evil* in Eden?

2. How are faith and risk related?

3. How would you respond to the charge that Christians are boring? Is God boring too?

4. What is the place of suffering in God's kingdom?

5. In what sense is God's glory ultimate?

SECTION IV

SORTING THROUGH PATHS TO FAITH

Chapter 8

Does It Matter What We Believe?

Everyone is entitled to their own opinion, but not their own facts.
—Daniel Patrick Moynihan

CONVICTIONS CHALLENGED

Global citizenship today is characterized by relativity, tolerance, and political correctness. Truth is treated as a relative concept, not an absolute reality. There's no right or wrong everything is relative. We are to be tolerant of all lifestyles even if it goes against the teachings of the Bible. We are to be politically correct by saying things in a way that pleases mainstream media. These are accepted behaviors expected of us. They are so well established, you wonder if there was a committee somewhere that decided these were the proper values for the modern person. When we live up to these expectations, we gain acceptance and are seen as good people. In the world's eyes, these values make us look good. They satisfy our longing to be liked.

Everyone wants to be liked. It is a basic human need to feel accepted by others. No one wants to be rejected. To be considered weird, strange, or from the dark ages, is often the alternative; and, few are willing to live with those labels.

Standing up for what honors God, when it goes against popular opinion, often draws those labels. It amounts to rejection in one form or another. And rejection carries with it a pain that can scar us for life. As a result, people crave acceptance and go to great lengths to avoid being shunned by others.

Unfortunately, the attention and effort spent avoiding 'stepping on toes' often come with the high price of sacrificing what we believe. That need we have to feel part of the in-crowd often threatens our need to hold on to our convictions. Howard Hendricks, one of last century's master teachers had been known to say, "A belief is something you argue about; a conviction is something you will die for." More and more, whether belief or conviction, few seems willing to stand for anything.

There is a movement of global proportions pressuring us to give-up our deepest convictions about anything. According to this popular and influential movement, we should not hold strong convictions. (The irony is that we are expected to *hold very tightly* to this popular way of thinking.) So, when our deep convictions are challenged as they often are, the politically correct thing to do is loosen our grip on them and give-in to the pressure to conform.

This philosophy argues that another's belief is just as valid as ours. We can believe anything we want as long as it is approved by the popular majority.

To say the least, those cherished values of relativity, tolerance, and political correctness can sometimes seem democratic; but is this sound advice? Will such a theory stand the test of time? Does each person's belief carry the same weight? Is there significant difference in the beliefs held from person to person? Does it matter what we believe?

IGNORING TRUTH WON'T MAKE IT GO AWAY

When I was a youth in my pre-teens, I would hear others say things that never seemed to make sense. For instance, some kids said that they didn't believe in evil spirits, so evil spirits couldn't harm them. They thought that their belief had some mystical power to render ineffective that which made them uncomfortable. When I was invited to their homes by the kindness of their parents, I noticed that their beliefs weren't merely the result of a kid's overactive imagination, but those of seasoned adults. They got those beliefs from their parents.

Some individuals under the influence of mind-altering, illegal drugs do not believe harm will come to them if they leap off a fifty-story high-rise. But the law of gravity does not stop working simply because people believe it does not exist— even during moments of temporary insanity. Ignoring it would not make it go away. It was James Russell Lowell who said,

> There is no good in arguing with the inevitable. The only argument available with an east wind is to put on your overcoat.

What about things which do not require the suspension of natural or supernatural laws? Does it really matter if we believe that all roads lead to the same God or that there is only one narrow way to the one true God? (This question is pursued further in the next chapter.) Is there really a difference whether I believe that life begins at conception or at some later time? Should it be so hotly debated whether those who are pro-choice or pro-life got it right? Should the cliché, "To each his own!" apply unconditionally to our beliefs?

Of course, merely believing something doesn't make it true as in the case of the drug addict plunging to his death. Neither were the laws of nature altered to accommodate his temporary state of insanity, nor were the supernatural laws suspended to nullify the existence of evil spirits.

THE NARROW NATURE OF TRUTH

Truth is, by definition, exclusive. It is not relative, it cannot be. It is narrow by nature. There must, of necessity, be a standard; and that is what constitutes truth.

The symbols used in the English language must mean something, to at least two people, for them to be able to communicate. The words must represent a given concept if there is to be some notion of sense.

First of all, each person participating in a conversation must share commonality with the chosen language. This is usually settled by the time children are five years old. By then, they have a working vocabulary and have understood enough of the rules to engage in conversation. Anyone making up their own rules cannot be a participant. Of course, there are variations to that commonality or theme; but, there must be a theme in the first place for variations to exist.

It is interesting to note the colorful varieties of spoken accents and dialects associated with the English language. In the United States alone, scores of accents may be heard in any reasonably sized city. Some of the better known accents may include those of New England, those in the North of the country, the Southerners, those in the West Coast, the East Coast, New York, Texas, African-Americans, Jewish-Americans, Italian-Americans, Caribbean-Americans, and the list is endless.

Ask five different people from around the country how they pronounce the term "Aunt," and you may end up with five distinct pronunciations. Some emphasize the <u>Au</u> in Aunt; others pronounce it with no distinction from the insect, Ant; some seem to drag out the word by adding extra "N's" like Annnnt; and so on.

Outside the United States, there are varieties in dialects and accents across the globe. In England, Scotland, Ireland, Wales, Africa, India and the West Indies many people speak English as their primary language—all of these with a slightly different nuance but recognizably English. Although there are many different variations on the theme, for any English speaking person to be able to comprehend and communicate with another, there must be a theme or a standard to begin with. Participants must agree upon the basics—the constants, those things that are non-negotiable, those things that are responsible for making it what it is. There must be standardization. It cannot be relative. Nothing seems to illustrate this better than an incident which occurred at my home.

SITTING ON A SCORPION?

An acquaintance of mine visited me at home one day and advocated this notion that there is no such thing as objective truth, "everything," he asserted, "is relative." He rationalized that he had his truth and I had mine. After offering him a seat, I asked him why he was sitting on a scorpion. Jumping to his feet and frantically shaking off his pants offered sufficient evidence that the words I used registered in his mind with the same meaning I intended. They were not relative at all. They did not have one meaning for me and a different meaning for him. He accurately interpreted the intended meaning. I then humored him with his line of reasoning,

> "What you call a chair, I call a scorpion. It is not a chair to me," I offered, "It is a scorpion. I have my truth, you have yours. It is all relative."

Somehow he did not seem to appreciate me referring to a wooden, four-legged piece of furniture with a backrest, a scorpion. If something is, it is; calling it something else doesn't make it something else. Any movement away from the theme, or standard (and I am not referring to a variation but a total shift) is playing dangerously with deception, falsehood, and lies.

BELIEVING THE WRONG THING CAN BE DEADLY

Lies are dangerous. No one walks into believing a lie with their eyes wide open. They have to be deceived and unaware that they are being fooled. That's what deception is, isn't it? We don't realize it is happening when it is in fact taking place. So we have to be all the more careful because innocence and ignorance do not shield the naïve from the consequences of deception. Naivety and blind faith can incur the ultimate cost.

The followers of Jim Jones who drank poisoned Kool-Aid to their deaths in Guyana, South America during the

1970's, paid the ultimate price for believing a lie. Because they believe their leaders have a special connection to God, followers of religious cults live a life of bondage. During the mediaeval age, witches were burnt at the stake. The mere accusation of being a witch brought the ultimate penalty— death. In these and countless other cases, people's lives were directly affected by what they believed.

This reality is not only critical when the consequences are obviously grave as is apparent in the above mentioned cases. It is also crucial in ordinary everyday choices made by well-intentioned and sincere people all across this globe. Most parents around the world lovingly nurture their children with the beliefs and values they cherish.

Christian parents raise their children to put their faith in Jesus Christ to secure eternal salvation. Hindu parents guide their families to practice the virtues of the Hindu culture/faith. Buddhists parents likewise teach their children to respect and observe the teachings of Buddha. The same may be said of Confucianism, Islam, Zen Buddhism, and countless belief systems.

No one would be justified in suggesting that these are not genuine, sincere, loving, even sacrificial efforts to raise loved ones. But do sincerity, love, and sacrifice make something true? Absolutely not! Truth is truth and falsehood is falsehood. We must be careful to believe the truth.

EITHER ... OR

The Bible proclaims that Jesus is the one and only unique Son of God, and that upon Him alone shall we place our faith if we are to receive forgiveness of sins and be fit for His presence in heaven. The Hindu religion says that Jesus is only one of many ways to heaven.

Now as tolerant, politically correct, and as relative as we may want to be, these two belief systems cannot be both right. They cannot be harmonized and coexist together without contradicting each other. At least one has to be wrong. It is either that the Bible is wrong and Jesus is a liar or a lunatic; or, it is right. But it can't be both. This is in total contradiction to the notion that Jesus *and* other gods may be worshiped.

But if the Hindu teachings are right then the Bible is wrong. They cannot both be right. Assuming the Bible is the absolute truth, but you believe the Hindu system negating the Bible's claims, the consequences would be everlasting punishment. But if the Hindu way is the correct way, and you believe the Bible, you are not in any real danger because according to them you can still find enlightenment.

BELIEF AFFECTS EVERYTHING

The fact is, what we believe matters so much that it drives everything we do. The path our lives take, and what we ultimately become, largely depends upon what we believe. That is, belief precedes action. Better yet, belief persuades action.

Nature vs. Nurture Debate

This, of course, is not a foregone conclusion for everyone. There is an ongoing debate about what is responsible for a person's behavior and lifestyle. Some call it the nature versus nurture debate. It is essentially a dispute about faith versus fate.

Is there some trait found in a person's DNA, which is responsible for what a person does? Or, do people's behavior and lifestyle depend upon the choices they make? Are the results of my life in my hands to the extent that I make responsible or irresponsible choices, or are they completely out of my control altogether? To ask the question another way, when people arrive at the choices they make, did their genetic code compel them to make those choices or did they arrive at their choices based upon the influence of their surrounding environment?

There are those who believe that people do what they do because of genetic fate or divine fate. They are convinced that they have no choice in the matter. They are persuaded that they possess a gene for say, alcoholism and there is nothing anyone can do to prevent them from becoming an alcoholic. There is no amount of belief, they argue, that can steer such a person away from his addictive fate. But the truth is, the choices we make affect what we do and become; and those choices are made based upon what we believe.

Self-Fulfilling Prophecy

Unknowingly, many who subscribe to that line of thinking invoke another phenomenon, the self-fulfilling prophecy.

This concept says that what a person expects (believes), materializes. A common example might be the parent who keeps telling her daughter that she is intelligent. When the daughter encounters difficulty in school and in life, because she believes that she is intelligent, she tries to analyze the problem and arrive at a viable solution, thus fulfilling the prophecy.

The converse is equally true. When parents and teachers repeatedly tell the young in their care that they are stupid, after a while these impressionable young people believe it and consequently act out the low expectations of those responsible for them. What we believe affects everything we do.

Our Faith in Others Helps Them

This scenario is played out in thousands of homes and educational institutions across the globe on a daily basis.

I have encountered students who were told all their lives that they weren't going to amount to anything. They were advised to drop out of school and learn a skill that doesn't require formal education. Somehow they ended up in our classrooms. We go to work on these students armed with informed faith. One of the most important things we bring to their lives is our belief in their ability to succeed in college and in life. Our faith in them is not a blind, wishful faith; it is an informed, evidence-based faith. It is based on proven scientific data; their healthy, street-smart minds; and a belief in God's magnificent and resilient creation—humankind.

Because some of us came out of similar situations, that reality often proves to inform our faith the strongest. We believe in our students' capabilities so much that by patiently motivating, encouraging, and challenging them to excellence, we graduate individuals who have come to believe in their own abilities and have become equipped for success.

At some point they themselves begin to believe and awaken the giant of success which had been asleep within them for years. Like an onion, the layers of self-doubt, misdirected criticisms, crushed spirits and despair had to be stripped away and replaced with the truth that they can be successful.

Belief Breaks Down Barriers

What people believe is critical to their success or failure in life. The argument may be made that we are greatly influenced, if not controlled, by what we believe. Of course no amount of faith could make the untrue, true. Believing that God does not exist doesn't make Him go away. It may, however, make us live as though He didn't exist—a decision that carries with it grave repercussions.

Maybe this is another reason God prized the avenue of faith to engage us. Having believed in Him, all barriers to worship are dismantled. Believers are free to give themselves to Him unrestrained, as one fully submits his will to God and worships Him. Belief in God opens up within us that window of communication and relationship building that might otherwise be closed.

Belief Affects our Jobs

Belief is pivotal to the success of any venture. People, who believe they possess the tools to do their jobs, approach their duties with confidence, boldness, positive anticipation, and less stress than those who are not equipped with similar faith. On the contrary, when people lack belief in their ability to do their jobs, they operate under an inordinate amount of stress and find little joy in their jobs. This, of course, is not fertile soil for success. In fact, many seek jobs which match their belief in their abilities.

There was an occasion when I had been summoned to my superior's office. Often when this happens we do not know what to think. It could be good news or it could be bad news. This time however, the mystery was short-lived as she readily introduced the purpose for our meeting. The following year there were to be some anticipated changes at our college. Her opening remarks directed to me were framed as a question, Are you ready to lead? This was an inquiry into my belief in my own abilities. Corporations do not want employees who don't have confidence in their own abilities. They understand that their success depends upon their employees' belief in themselves.

Belief Governs Our Peace

Every decision we make is first filtered through our belief system. There is a sense in which we all live by a measure of faith. For some, it may not be faith in God, but faith in something, whatever it is. We cannot, not have faith.

We can however, make decisions which go against what we believe. When we do, we experience a measure of confusion because we violated our conscience. We knew better but didn't do better. We lied to ourselves. We may even mentally construct a verbal defense in anticipation of possible challenges from impending accusers. And we are usually fully aware when this is happening. Many people who believe it is wrong to cheat on an exam will resort to cheating if they deem it important to their success and if they believe the risk of being found out is low. They lie to themselves and suffer the effects of an unhappy and disturbed soul. But when we do the things which parallel our beliefs, no confusion is created; rather, confidence, normalcy, and peace permeate our beings.

Belief Transforms Our Lives

Strong evidence that our belief matters is shown in its ability to transform lives. And there may be no clearer picture of faith's power to transform than the tremendous change in Jesus' disciples after His resurrection. Peter's outright denial that he was part of Jesus' group (Matthew 26:73-74) highlights the crippling fear which gripped all the disciples prior to Jesus' crucifixion. "No! I don't know Him!" Peter protested. He even resorted to using obscene language to remove any doubt from the minds of his accusers.

But all that fear of being associated with Jesus during His arrest and crucifixion turned into bold, confident, faith after His resurrection. Armed with a renewed and relentless belief, Peter and the disciples, not only identified with Jesus, but counted it an honor to suffer persecution for His sake (Acts 5:41). History records that Peter was persecuted for believing in Jesus. We're told that he asked to be crucified upside-down because he felt unworthy to die like his Lord. What a transformation their faith had on them.

So does it matter what we believe? What we believe is critical to our survival and happiness. It matters more what we truly believe than what we say we believe. We find meaning and fulfillment based on what we believe. Joy and peace result from a life anchored in faith in our Creator. Belief transforms us.

CHAPTER 8 DISCUSSION QUESTIONS

1. In what ways are Christian convictions challenged in contemporary society?

2. How would you respond to the charge that truth is relative?

3. How does the Bible's uniqueness shed light on the importance of what we believe?

4. What are some major things that faith affects?

Chapter 9

Do All Roads
Lead To The Same God?

*There is a way which seems right to a man,
but its end is the way of death.*

—Proverbs 14:12

One of the most prevalent beliefs today is that all roads lead to the same God. The idea is that God presents Himself in many different forms making access to Him possible through many different religions. According to this common belief, people may connect with God through their god of choice; Jehovah, Jesus, Allah, Krishna, Vishnu, and Buddha to mention a few well-known names.

This belief also says we may find God through Christianity, Islam, Hinduism, Judaism, Rastafarianism, Buddhism and any other religion. We are told that it does not matter which belief we adopt, they are all basically the same, "All roads lead to the same God; all religions lead to the same place."

But is that true? Does each religious path take us to the same God? Will we end up the same place regardless of which god we worship?

Many ideas seem sensible and reasonable to us especially when they are popular and everyone is parroting the same thing. They are often passed off as proven, acceptable fact when in reality they are not proven at all. You would agree that most fail to stop and think about these popular clichés that gets thrown around as if they were absolute truth.

An easy-to-recognize one might be that "Money is the root of all evil." Yet those who use that popular line are twisting its meaning by misquoting what was originally said. The correct statement is,

> The *love of money* is the root of all evils.
>
> —1 Timothy 6:10

When you think of it, money is not evil at all; it is neither good nor bad, it is neutral. Money is an innocent tool to be used in exchange for the wholesome goods and services we all need. But when people love money so much that they are willing to compromise their moral and ethical standards and violate their conscience to get it, their greed leads to evil deeds.

So greed (which is the *love* of money) is the root of all evil because it puts me and my agenda above all else. Greed is the epitome of self-centeredness and self-serving behavior and leads to all kinds of evil deeds. If we take a moment to stop and think through statements like these, we may develop a healthy fear of arriving at wrong conclusions simply because those statements sound good to us and have popular support.

And one of those popular ideas floating around is that all roads lead to the same God. This idea may appeal to us because we get to choose which religion we like. We get to be the ones in control and not God, whom we can't see, telling us He's right. But the great concern is whether that road leads to peace. It is tempting to jump on the bandwagon without questioning its ability to get us to the destination we seek. But before we buy-in to the belief that all roads lead to the same God, let us take out our magnifying glasses and look carefully at its foundation. The stakes are too high to overlook.

MANY WAYS TO GOD THEORY COMES UP SHORT

While on the surface the many ways to God theory may be appealing, it is riddled with inconsistencies and contradictions. And God cannot contradict Himself. One thing that must be consistent with God if He were to manifest Himself in different ways is His essence. He cannot be contradictory to who He is and still be who He is. Yet, this is exactly what we are being asked to accept from those who advocate the notion that all roads lead to the same God.

Other Deities Contradictory to the God of the Bible

Assuming that the God of the Bible is the true and living God, we find that although many people claim that Allah, for instance, is just another name for (Yahweh) the God of the Bible, the descriptions of the two are very different. Well known religions like Islam, Jehovah Witnesses, Judaism, and Hinduism, stand in opposition to Yahweh and His ways. God cannot be speaking from both sides of His mouth, saying one thing in the Bible and contradicting Himself in the Quran. It is clear that Allah is very different from Yahweh.

The Bible's Description of God

The Bible describes God as existing in three expressions (or persons) Father, Son, and Holy Spirit. These are not three different gods; they are one God (Deuteronomy 6:4) manifest in three (Matthew 28:19)—notice the singular "name," not names. The Father is neither greater than the Son nor Holy Spirit, neither is the Holy Spirit any less God than the Son and Father; they are equally God.

Many have attempted to provide helpful explanations of this Trinity mystery. God's revelation of Himself to us is just that a mystery. But it is by no means unreasonable.

Some have used ice, water, and steam as an example of one substance manifest in three different forms. Others have suggested the tripartite nature of humans being body, soul, and spirit, illustrates trinity. I recently heard one member of identical twins describe her sister and herself as basically one person with different personalities. I know they were produced from one human egg.

Although this is difficult for the human mind to grasp it is the Bible's declaration of God. God transcends human comprehension.

The Father is not the Son, the Son is not the Holy Spirit and the Holy Spirit is not the Father, yet; the Father is God, the Son is God and the Holy Spirit is God. Each member of the Trinity is distinct yet there is a united possession of attributes, nature, and purposes. And none other is God but these three-in-one. All three persons of the Godhead are responsible for creating all things, giving life to all, are worshiped by men and all three accept worship from people and angels. The Father does not get jealous when the Son and Spirit are worshiped and vice versa.

Since the deity of the Father is usually unquestioned, and the Holy Spirit may be more easily understood as God, we turn our attention to the deity of Jesus Christ, the Son.

1. Jesus Creates the Earth—Demonstrates Deity

As a member of the Godhead, Jesus is credited with the creation of all things. The first line of the Bible reads, "In the beginning God created the heavens and the earth." The word translated God here is the generic plural word Elohim for God. This plurality included the Father, Son, and Holy Spirit who, as Genesis went on to declare, created all things. Still in context of creating the earth, the very next verse says,

> . . . the Spirit of God hovered over the waters.
>
> —Genesis 1:3

The Holy Spirit is doing what only God can do—create.

John was more explicit when he introduced Jesus. From the onset he tells his readers that Jesus is God, the creator of all things. Referring to Him by one of His titles, *The Word,* John proclaimed,

> In the beginning was the Word and the Word was with God and the Word was God . . . *All things came into being through Him, and without Him nothing came into being that came into being* ... And the Word became flesh and lived among us. And we saw His Glory, the glory as of the only begotten of the Father full of grace and truth.
>
> —John 1:1, 3, 14

Of course, this Word by whom all things were made and who became flesh, is Jesus—God the Son.

2. Jesus Accepts Worship—Demonstrates Deity

Worship is meant for God alone. Sometimes when people witnessed the power of God in the presence of His prophets, apostles, and angels they were so impressed that they bowed down in worship to them. But their worship was rejected; instead, the worshippers were directed to worship God to whom worship rightfully belongs.

In Acts 10:25-26 Cornelius bowed prostrate to worship the apostle Peter.

> But Peter raised him up saying, 'Stand up; I too am just a man.

Another time the apostles Paul and Barnabas were in the ancient Greek city of Lystra. After Paul healed a citizen there, the people were so impressed with the instant improvement that they began treating them like gods. They called Paul, Hermes, and Barnabas, Zeus. But Paul replied to them,

> Men, why are you doing these things? We are also men of the same nature as you . . . turn from these vain things to the living God who made the heavens and the earth and the sea and all that is in them.
> —Acts 14: 15

A third example involves a time John the apostle encountered an angel of God. Impressed by its magnificence he fell down to offer worship. Here again the angel said,

> Do not do that; I am a fellow servant of yours and your brethren who hold the testimony of Jesus; worship God.
> —Revelation 19:10; 22:9

Peter, Paul, Barnabas, and the angel all recognized that they were mere agents of God. They weren't confused about their identities. They served at God's bidding. They were fellow worshippers of God and were not themselves to be worshiped.

But this pattern was curiously broken when people worshiped Jesus; He didn't tell them to stop it, He received it. In John 20:27-28, after He rose from the dead, Jesus invited the disciple Thomas to examine the crucifixion nail holes in His hands and feet and the wound left by the spear in His side. Upon Thomas' careful scrutiny of the risen Christ he cried out,

My Lord and my God!

Jesus' response to that was,

Because you have seen me you have believed? Blessed are those who did not see and yet believe.

Interestingly, Jesus did not say that He was just a man; He accepted Thomas' worship because He was God.

Of course, merely accepting worship does not prove deity. The Caesars of Rome intoxicated themselves with the godlike status they paraded before their citizens and basked in the worship they demanded of them. This, of course, is extremely dangerous. For, God does not share His glory with anyone. He is not pleased when people accept worship.

I am the Lord, that is My name; I will not give My glory to another, nor My praise to graven images.

—Isaiah 42:8

Luke, who wrote Acts, tells us about the time a Roman ruler accepted worship and paid the ultimate price.

> On a day determined in advance, Herod put on his royal robes, sat down on the judgment seat, and made a speech to them. But the crowd began to shout, 'The voice of a god, and not of a man!' Immediately an angel of the Lord struck Herod down because he did not give the glory to God, and he was eaten by worms and died.
>
> —Acts 12:21-23

Jewish historian Josephus (A.D. 37-A.D. 100), who lived at the time, reported that Herod wore a silver robe that day capturing the sun's dazzling reflection and showing himself god-like (Josephus, Ant. 19.8.2). But God, who is patient, had enough of that behavior and showed everyone that He had power over Herod's life.

Everything about Jesus points directly to His divinity.

Many other religions distance themselves from the God of the Bible on this very issue. Their followers find it problematic acknowledging Jesus as God. Yet Jesus' deity cannot be compromised.

Muslims have reduced Jesus to a mere prophet. They will grant that He was a prophet but certainly not God. Judaism refers to Jesus as an imposter; they do not revere Him even as their messiah—certainly not God. Jehovah Witnesses say He is *a god* but certainly not *God*. Hindus will include Jesus among their pantheon of gods. To them, He is merely one among millions of other gods.

Those contradict the Bible's description of God. They do not have the same essence. Their gods are very different. It is not the same God to whom all roads may lead. Those roads lead to deities distinct from the God of the Bible.

John the apostle wrote to raise our awareness of the various spirits claiming to be God. He issued warnings against the popular notion that all roads lead to the same God when he wrote,

> Beloved, do not believe every spirit, but test the spirits to see whether they are from God; because many false prophets have gone out into the world. By this you know the Spirit of God: every spirit that confesses that Jesus Christ has come in the flesh is from God . . . .
>
> —1 John 4:1-3

There is that language again . . . the Word becoming flesh, Jesus Christ is come in the flesh.

3. Father calls Son, God— Demonstrates Deity

A third observation which demonstrates that Jesus is fully God comes to light when He is called God by God the Father. In Hebrews 1:8 the author quotes Psalms 45:6 revealing that God the Father referred to the Son as God.

> But of the Son He says, thy throne oh God is forever and ever, a scepter of righteousness is a scepter of thy kingdom.

Here God the Father refers to God the Son as God!

Recognizing that throughout the Holy Scriptures the Father, Son, and Holy Spirit manifest qualities belonging only to God, Bible scholars coined the useful term, "Trinity," to refer to the triune God. This unique, Holy Trinity works in absolute harmony to accomplish their purposes. We have already seen all three work together in creation. A similar involvement is undertaken when it comes to the spiritual salvation of mankind.

The Father planned humanity's spiritual salvation; the Son paid for it with His death on the cross; and the Spirit preserves our salvation. Because Jesus physically showed up on our planet and purchased our redemption when He laid down His sinless life on the cross just two thousand years ago, He is the portal through whom we have access to God. Referring to Jesus, we read in Acts 4:12 that,

> There is no other name under heaven given among men by which we must be saved.

Jesus Himself, when He prayed to His father before He went to the cross, uttered these words,

> Now this is eternal life—that they know You, the only true God and Jesus Christ, whom You sent.
>
> —John 17:3

According to the God of the Bible, no other road, way, religion, or deity is acceptable to Him. All roads do not lead to the same God.

The following chart shows the uniqueness of God as described in the Bible.

Attributes of God Evident in the Trinity			
Attribute	**Father**	**Son**	**Holy Spirit**
All Knowing	1 John 3:20	John 16:20; 21:17	1 Corinthians 2:10,11
Called God	Philippians 1:2	John 1:1-14; Col 2:9	Acts 5:3-4
Creator	Isaiah 64:8	John 1:3; Col 1:15-17	Job 33:4; 26:13
Eternal	Psalm 90:2	Micah 5:1-2; John 8:58	Rom 8:11; Heb 9:14
Everywhere	1 Kings 8:27	Matthew 18:20; 28:20	Psalm 139:7-10
Life Giver	Gen 2:7; John 5:21	John 1:3; 5:21	2 Corinthians 3:6,8
Resurrects	1Thessalonians 1:10	John 2:19; 10:17	Romans 8:11
Searches Hearts	Jeremiah 17:10	Revelation 2:23	1 Corinthians 2:10

MRS. GUPTA

I had the privilege of meeting my friend's mother a few years ago. She was moving in to live with him and his family. Any opportunity to meet her sooner was lost since she previously lived in another country. My friend Ravi believed the gospel of Christ but wanted me to know that his mother did not believe in Jesus the way the Bible calls us to believe in Him. He explained that when he was growing up, he was taught to believe that Jesus was only one of many ways to God. And Ravi's mom, Mrs. Gupta, held strong faith in what she called enlightenment practices.

After being introduced to Mrs. Gupta, it wasn't long before we entered into a full-blown discussion on matters of spiritual importance. The tasty chai which usually accompany those conversations still lingers on in my memory as did our engaging chat. Mrs. Gupta was confident, assertive, and forceful. As she put it,

> I am going to convert each person I meet; and teach them how to achieve a state of enlightenment.

It is safe to say she was on a mission. Naturally, since I had a keen interest in questions of eternal consequences, I looked

171

forward to our discussion with great interest. I kept an open mind. It makes absolutely no sense to me to enter into any discussion with the assumption that I already have all the answers.

Mrs. Gupta talked at length about enlightenment. She believed that by letting go of desire, people can achieve a state of enlightenment and even nirvana (peace, paradise, heaven). After a lengthy discussion over the question of what brings true inner peace, I was curious to know what was driving this lady whose ambition it was to convert everyone she met to her way of thinking. I admired her resolve to pass on to others what she believed, what she held near and dear to her heart. And I wondered how her views might be different if she applied an informed approach to her faith.

Her basic belief was that there are many gods and that millions of gods are around us every day. To her way of thinking, every living being was practically a god of one kind or another. God can appear in many different ways and have appeared to various civilizations under different names suitable to each unique culture. So if God appeared to a certain group of people, that god will show them how to find peace and be on good terms with him or her. And the way to peace will be different from god to god and group to group.

Now, when people say that God gave Confucianism, Buddhism, and Hinduism to the Asians, Islam to the people in the middle-east, Judaism to the Jews, African religions to the Africans, and Christianity to the Westerners it may seem fair and reasonable. While on the other hand, they accuse biblical Christianity of being narrow and exclusive to only Christians. As a result, it may appear unfair and unreasonable to ask someone who was raised in China, let's say, which has over one billion people or India, which also has a population in excess of a billion, to trust in Jesus Christ for the forgiveness of their sins. They may think, in fact some have told me,

> I have my own religion, why do I have to believe in Jesus Christ? He is the Christian's God. I have my own!

Although that widely accepted belief may, on the surface appear to be reasonable, it overlooks several important things.

ONE WAY FOR EVERYBODY

One important consideration it overlooks is that it makes perfect sense that God provided only one way to Him. It is neither unfair nor unreasonable for the Supreme One to have His creatures approach Him through the way He provided them. By nature and by definition, God is the one who gets to make up the rules for everything, for how the universe runs and the rules of life and death. The Bible's account that God provided us His Son Jesus Christ, and calls upon the world to believe in Him, makes wholesome sense. When Jesus Christ showed up on earth as a baby, lived a pure life and died for the sins of the world, His sacrificial death was not for the benefit of Christians alone or for westerners alone. Christ died for every person in the world. Referring to Jesus, the apostle John had this to say.

> He Himself is the propitiation (atoning sacrifice) for our sins, and not only for our sins but also for the whole world.
>
> —1 John 2:2

Paul the apostle stood before a very religious and educated group of philosophers at the Areopagus on Mars Hill, in Athens, Greece and declared:

> The God who made the world and everything in it, who is Lord of heaven and earth . . . He Himself gives life and breath and everything to everyone. From one man He made every nation of the human race to inhabit the entire earth, determining their set times and the fixed limits of places where they would live, so they would search for God and perhaps grope around for Him and find Him, though He is not far from each one of us.
>
> —Acts 17: 24-27

God created us all and His remedy for our biggest problem, sin, is His Son's sinless sacrifice. He is not the Christians' God alone; He is the God of all cultures and peoples. His own words attest to this fact.

> And He said to them, "Thus it is written, that the Christ should suffer and rise again from the dead the third day; and that repentance for forgiveness of sins should be proclaimed in His name to all the nations, beginning from Jerusalem."
>
> —Luke 24:46-47

Mrs. Gupta was able to receive this idea that God could have sent His Son Jesus to pay for the sins of the whole world, but she struggled with my next statement at first, until an example was used which proved hard for her to deny.

God's Understandable Jealousy

My next statement was,

The Bible declares that God is a jealous God and that although He has great patience, ultimately He has no tolerance for others claiming to be God or any who receive worship directed to them.

Worship belongs only to God. But Mrs. Gupta could not understand why God should be jealous. She said,

What does He have to be jealous about? If people found peace and satisfaction by worshipping someone or something else, why should that be of concern to Him?

Here again I have to admit that it sounds fair to live and let live; to be, and let be. That is one of the world's cherished values. And we all appreciate being free to choose how we wish to live our lives. But we are not simply talking about options of personal taste and personal preference here; we are talking about the Supreme One and His directives.

To help Mrs. Gupta understand God's jealousy, I used an example I knew she, as a mother, would identify with. I asked her how certain she was that Ravi was her child. Naturally, she was a bit surprised by my question. But after recovering from the shock of the question, she assured me that there was no possible way that Ravi was not her child. She not only remembers giving birth to him, she also recalled the entire pregnancy and how he used to kick while in the womb. As a matter of fact, she said she can pick him out from among the crowds in the city of Mumbai simply by the way he walks, even from a mile away. Mrs. Gupta talked about the type of child Ravi was and other little things a mother alone would know. She talked about taking care of him when he was sick, the things he likes, and that promising to make him his favorite porridge was the only way to get him to stop crying.

I listened and watched as this mother spoke with absolute certainty and deep affection for her son, Ravi. Then I asked the telling question.

How would you take it if some other woman came along and made serious claims to be Ravi's mother? Or, how would you like to see Ravi give his love and loyalty to another woman as his mother instead of to you?

I asked her to think about some other woman saying to her,

No, but this is my child. He never was yours and could never be yours. He is my son.

I asked her to picture her son clinging to that woman fully treating her as his mother.

To this day, I think she still has not forgiven me for asking those questions. You see, it is unthinkable for a mother to imagine her child being mothered by anyone else but herself.

Needless to say, I don't think Mrs. Gupta will ever struggle with the question of God's jealousy again.

God created each and every one of us. No other claiming to be God regardless of name or region can rightly hold that title or rightly deserve that reverence. As our Creator and Father, He alone gets the privileges of Creator and Father. This is the very essence of jealousy which is different from envy. Envy has to do with desiring someone else's possession; whereas, jealousy rises in our hearts when someone else threatens to steal what belongs to us. So it is perfectly plausible that God sent His one and only unique Son Jesus Christ to die a sacrificial death for the sins of every person in the world. And it is naturally expected that He would have no tolerance for others claiming to be God.

> He alone is God and besides Him there is none else.
> —Isaiah 43:11; 44:6; 45:5-6

After our discussion, Mrs. Gupta was willing to consider the possibility that God may have provided only one way to Him. It makes perfect sense that since God created us, ANY OTHER gods or religions accepting worship are frauds. ANY OTHER way except God's provision through Jesus Christ will be nothing less than the ugliest insult thrown at Him. Maybe the apostle John said it best in his epistle.

> If we receive the witness of men, the witness of God is greater; for the witness of God is this, that He has borne witness concerning His Son.
> —1 John 5:9

This takes us back to the time when the Lord Jesus Christ walked this earth with His disciples in Israel. At one point He asked His disciples "Who do men say that I am?" I believe He wanted to expose what was in the hearts and minds of the people concerning who He was. Who did they identify Him as? The disciples then began to tell Him what others were saying about Him. Some said He was the prophet Elijah; others, that He was John the Baptist; and still others, that He was one of the prophets of old now living again.

Then He turned the question on them, making it more personal, as if to say, "You've been around Me all this time and have seen and heard Me. What do you say? Who do you think I am?" And Peter, as their spokesperson, blurted out "The Christ, the Son of the living God."

Eight days later Jesus took three of His disciples Peter, James, and John up to a mountain to pray. While He was praying, His appearance changed. His face became different and His clothing became white and shinning. This event has since been called the transfiguration. He was transfigured right before their eyes. When Peter saw it, not knowing what to say, he said something inappropriate. Then a voice spoke from a cloud which overshadowed them and said,

> This is My beloved Son. My chosen One. Listen to Him!
> —Matthew 17:5; Mark 9:7; Luke 9:35

So I join in with the apostle John to say, if we receive the witness of men, the witness of God is greater. Men said He was a prophet. His disciples said He was the Christ or Messiah, the anointed One. But God said He is His Son. And as His Son, He is the only way to God.

CHAPTER 9 DISCUSSION QUESTIONS

1. What is society's attitude to the idea that, "All roads lead to the same God?"

2. How does God being a jealous God shed light on the idea that one way to God is plausible?

3. In what ways is it reasonable that one way to God makes sense?

4. What are some contradictions which debunk the notion that we are all worshipping the same God?

THE INNER WORKINGS OF FAITH

Chapter 10

What Makes Faith Work?

It is not the strength of your faith but the object of your faith that actually saves you.

—Timothy Keller

FAITH IN FAITH?

Where does faith get its punch? What causes it to move mountains and change lives? Is it self-generating? Does it depend upon a source outside itself? When attempting to understand these fundamental questions, two separate ideas have emerged—

1. Faith in itself, and
2. Faith in someone or something else.

Many people place their faith in faith rather than placing their faith in a person, an idea, or an object. That is, they exert effort and labor upon generating as much faith as they can when trying to win favor with God.

In a typical evangelistic scene, the evangelist presents the claims of Christ to a skeptical audience. Convinced seekers are made to understand that belief is a requirement for salvation. They have been told that it takes faith to make the leap from sinner to saint. So, they believe. Weeks later some who believed show no signs that any real changes took place. Others exhibit vibrant excitement about their newfound life. What's the difference between the two groups?

Nigel and Melody are members of the same church and both attend the adult Bible class. They both expressed a desire for promotion on their jobs but take different routes to achieve their goals. Nigel does everything in his power to secure the promotion. He is a competent employee, always on time for work, and has put in the required number of years of experience. He also prays to God for the promotion and is content to wait upon Him to grant his request in His own time. He remains at peace and waits on the Lord as he continues to be a good employee.

Melody is also competent at her job and does all the proper things befitting a promotion-worthy employee. She also believes she will get the promotion because she has faith. Melody however, grows increasingly frustrated as the months pass by and no promotion has been granted her. What is the difference between the two?

FAITH'S OBJECT

In the preceding scenarios, a common and misleading misconception is at work regarding the placement of one's faith. *Faith works, not because it has any intrinsic power to deliver, but because it is backed by something or someone with the ability to deliver. In other words, faith is powerless in-and-of itself. It is the object of one's faith that gives faith its power. It is the entity faith is placed in that empowers it.* If faith's object has power to deliver, then placing confidence in it is likely to produce results; conversely, when faith's object lacks the ability to produce, no results may be expected.

When investors seek a safe financial vehicle to invest their treasured earnings, they have various levels of security at their disposal. The stock market is volatile (risky), the bond market is more stable, and US government bonds are very safe. All three of these vehicles carry with them a measure of risk but the US government bonds are the safest. That is because the bonds can fail to deliver only if the American government dissolves itself or goes bankrupted. If an investor is seeking security for his funds, one of his safest places will be the US government bonds. Since the United States government is stable enough and powerful enough to deliver on their promises they are the safest choice for investors.

When unbelievers trust God's provision for their sins they enjoy the assurance that they will be in heaven when they die because it is impossible for God to fail, die, forget, lie, or break His promises. There abides a growing sense of confidence, contentment and security because the object of their faith is the infallible God and not merely faith itself. It is God who does the saving not faith. Faith is the vehicle by which God saves. Such faith must sit squarely upon the finished work of Jesus Christ.

Melody experienced frustration because her faith rested in her faith or herself—she trusted in her own ability to produce faith—not in God's ability to deliver. What real power did she have to guarantee the results she craved? If the truth is told, none whatsoever! She could only do so much and no more. God doesn't honor that kind of self-reliance; He honors faith in Him, not because He is egotistical, but because He is the only one who can make things happen.

Nigel experienced peace and contentment because his faith rested upon God to answer in His own time.

> Imagine a ship filled with people crossing the Atlantic. In the middle of the ocean there is an explosion. The ship is severely damaged and slowly sinking. Most are dead, and the rest are rushing for the lifeboats . . . [Some] *believe* the lifeboat will save them, and they get into the boat. They are saved by faith . . . However, it is not their faith that saves them—no matter how much they have. It is the boat. Saving faith trusts Christ, and Christ saves (Cocoris, 1984, p. 77).

FEELINGS VS. GOD'S WORD

My own spiritual journey takes me back to a time in my youth when I grappled with similar questions. How did I know if my faith was working? Did I have enough faith? Mine was a question of assurance. How did I *know* if I possessed eternal life? Did I ever have it? Did I receive it and somehow lost it somewhere along the way? In other words, did my faith work? Having a healthy respect for the duration of eternity, these unanswered questions provided no relief to my worried mind.

One day I brought this burden to an elderly man who was noted for his Bible knowledge and piety. Mr. Edgar King must have been in his seventies; I would have been in my early teens at the time. But I recall the conversation as if it were yesterday. A frail man with a gentle and reassuring presence about him, Mr. King appears in my memory with a humble servant-hearted demeanor. He could be seen inching ahead from pew to pew at snail's pace restacking the hymnals left lying around at the conclusion of each church service.

The friendly chatter of a homely church family perfumed the cool Caribbean night. But I had a troubling question on my mind. After exchanging the customary greetings and selecting a secluded seat near the rear, I launched my inquiry, the large dark mahogany pews swallowing up my tiny frame.

"Brother King" (we referred to all the church members as brothers and sisters) "How do I know if I have everlasting life?"

Taking a deep breath, he thought for a moment before he replied, "Well, have you believed on Jesus Christ?"

I responded, "Yes I believe in Jesus."

His follow-up question was immediate, his voice nimble but sure as it was purposeful. "What does the Bible say is the way to eternal life?"

My response was equally immediate, 'Everyone knew the answer to that,' I thought to myself: "To believe in Jesus!"

His next reply at first didn't seem especially helpful. "Then what is the problem?" he asked.

I reminded him that I knew what the Bible said but my question remained, "How do I *know* if I have everlasting life?"

Brother King patiently asked me again, "Have you believed in Jesus? Do you trust in Him for your salvation?"

Again I responded (this time out of frustration) "Yes sir, I have, and I do!" I glanced up at him and noticed that he was wearing a smile of contentment, as his eyes searched my expression for clues that he might be getting through.

Then it happened. It suddenly became clear to me as if it had always been obvious. I was expecting my faith to be strong because I thought *the feeling of strong faith* would mean I had been given eternal life. But there were moments when I didn't quite feel that my faith in Jesus was working. In fact, my request for our one-on-one chat was due to one of those moments when I wasn't particularly feeling quite secure about my faith. But he saw the confusion etched on my countenance and his repetition was meant to have me focus on what God said, not how I felt.

Aah! That was the missing piece of information. Brother King was pointing out to me that my eternal destiny didn't depend upon the way I felt at a given moment about my faith at all; for, feelings come and go. I may feel one way now about something but feel different at another moment about that same thing. It depended upon God—the object of my faith. Will God keep His word? Is He reliable? Does God possess the power to perform what He promised, thereby granting me eternal life? That is why brother King kept asking me, "What does the Bible say?" His point? God declared in the Bible that faith in Jesus Christ guarantees eternal life. I have faith in Jesus Christ therefore I have everlasting life.

I was careful thereafter to shift any trust I held in my own faith or in myself, over to Him where it rightfully belongs if it was to have any success. Doing that made the difference in my life of faith. I now see clear results because my faith is in God, not anywhere else. I have since learned to appreciate the Scripture found in 1 Corinthians 2:5 which states;

> Your faith should not rest in the wisdom of men, but in the power of God.

It is this distinction that makes all the difference. It is where one's faith rests that determines if it will have results.

ॐ

CHAPTER 10 DISCUSSION QUESTIONS

1. What common misapplication of faith do people make?

2. What gives faith its power?

Chapter 11

Must Faith Be Perfect To Work?

For He Himself knows our frame;
He is mindful that we are but dust.
—Psalm 103:14

FRUSTRATIONS OF FAILED FAITH

God requires faith, but how much faith does He require? What quality or quantity is sufficient? Must faith be free of all doubts before it can accomplish its intended purpose?

People around the world have struggled with these questions. Desperate and vulnerable hopefuls seeking healing from cancers, tumors, paralysis and a host of other ailments have left faith-healing sessions in frustration and with an even greater sense of desperation than they had prior to their encounter with faith-healers. Their burdens increase because they are told that the reason for their failed attempts at healing results from their lack of faith. How much is sufficient or how strong is strong? Must faith be perfect to work? The spotlight shines directly upon faith's fabric.

ABRAHAM'S EXAMPLE

It is doubtful that anyone upon the face of this globe can truthfully claim to possess perfect faith, that is, faith without ever questioning the outcome. The Bible refers to Abraham as the father of the faithful. As if to say, when you want to understand good, strong, solid, faith, look at Abraham. When an investigative searchlight beams into every corner of Abraham's life, one is not disappointed to discover evidence of remarkable faith. No serious student of the Bible trivializes the courage it takes to leave all and follow God into a country not knowing where you're going. Yet this was the ambiguous beginning Abraham managed with God. And there were instances when even Abraham appeared to have abandoned his faith, or at least, entertained questions of doubt in God's ability to deliver.

Recall the historical account? God promised Abraham that he would be the father of many nations. There was however, one problem: Abraham and his wife Sarah were old and past childbearing age. Sarah was barren; she was unable to conceive and have children. In this situation, Abraham can't even father one child let alone many nations. To solve this not-so-little problem, Sarah suggested that Abraham pursue God's promise illegitimately, by committing adultery with their maid, Hagar. What does the father of the faithful do? He listens to his wife instead of trusting in God to fulfill His promise to them.

Many people reading this well-known narrative, struggle to find any faith in Abraham's decision to try and help God fulfill His promise to them through the back door. But how does God view this display of faith? In Romans, that comprehensive treatment on the topic of the Gospel, God drops a shocker when He says of Abraham,

> With respect to the promise of God, he did not waver in unbelief, but grew strong in faith, giving glory to God.
> —Romans 4: 20

Although the ancient record shows that Abraham obviously blundered at that incident, God still said that he did not waver. His faith held firm.

WHAT ABOUT SMALL, IMPERFECT FAITH?

Faith does not have to be perfect to work or for it to gain God's approval otherwise no one will ever be able to please God. We are all imperfect. And the imperfect cannot produce perfection in any sense. This truth is nothing short of liberating. Although it is, to be sure, not to be confused as opportunity to abuse God's grace; it is wonderfully assuring that when we struggle with doubt in the face of impossible odds, we are not deemed failures. God still counts the trickles of faith mingled in with the moments of struggle.

In the New Testament, Jesus assured his audience that if they had as much faith as a mustard seed they could move mountains. Now a mustard seed is among the smallest of seeds. This does not glorify small faith; it asserts the power of faith, even if it is small. It was Dwight L. Moody, the persuasive and influential evangelist who said,

> A little faith will bring your soul to heaven, but a lot of faith will bring heaven to your soul.

All faith will work whether large or small.

On one occasion, Jesus had just chided His generation for their lack of faith and then stated that all things were possible to those who believe. Hearing this, a man whose son had been demon possessed cried out,

> I do believe; help my unbelief.
>
> —Mark 9:24

This resulted in his son's immediate healing.

Therefore it is not so much the amount of faith we possess; but, that we exercise the faith we have even with its imperfections.

✦

CHAPTER 11 DISCUSSION QUESTIONS

1. What does Abraham's example teach us about the nature of successful and unsuccessful faith?

Chapter 12

When Faith Doesn't Seem To Work

We will be victorious if we have not forgotten how to learn.
—Rosa Luxemburg

REMEMBER WHO GOD IS

There are times in every believer's life when they wonder if their faith is working. Many have exercised faith in God about a particular matter they have been praying about—healing from a life-threatening disease, their children's eternal salvation, to escape the ravages of poverty, to find a long lost relative, to meet and marry the partner of their dreams, for capital to start a health clinic or a school for needy children, and the list goes on and on. Sometimes people agonize with God in prayer for long periods of time and still end up with unsatisfying results.

But how are we to understand this lack of results? What would be the proper response to these disappointing circumstances? Is this evidence that faith doesn't always work? If God is indeed true to His Word, how can this reality experienced universally by virtually all believers be explained? Is there a breakdown in faith? Does faith always work? Is faith reliable? These questions hit at the very core of faith's integrity.

They strike at the heart of faith's honor. What is going on behind the scenes when faith doesn't seem to work?

To know if something is working or not it must be measurable. There must come a point in the process when we recognize it as either a success or a failure. And although we can trust in God for things without actually making a formal request through prayer, it is upon prayer we usually rely to gauge our faith-o-meter.

When we receive a favorable answer to a prayer, we say that our faith has worked. But questions arise when there are no positive answers. A clear-cut example of an all too familiar case may be the time when we are praying for a loved one who is on his deathbed. We earnestly pray from the depths of our beings for God to heal our loved one. We do not question God's ability to heal the illness and restore health to our family member but the worst happens in spite of our faith; our loved one dies anyway. Surely, our faith did not appear to work. Death was a clear-cut example because of its finality.

Other cases may be a bit more complicated to judge because of the time factor. Many people trust in God for say, healing from some disease. Years pass without any healing. Did their faith fail? Is it possible that their faith is working and healing is lurking just around the corner? How long should the requestor wait before concluding that faith has failed?

Any number of factors may be at work in a given situation. The first and overriding thing we must never forget is that God is the Supreme Being. Accepting this may account for how we view successful faith and failed faith. He is the only true Sovereign. All power belongs to Him. He is the one in charge of all things. He dictates to us, not the other way around.

Some people may sincerely and earnestly pray to God for months requesting say, reliable transportation to get to and from work and no answer has come. Absolutely nothing may be wrong with the person's faith. The problem may lie, neither with God nor with the quality of their faith, but with their expectations. As we've seen in the previous chapter, the apparent failure of faith in the believer's life often draws the accusation that one did not possess enough faith.

But this widespread notion fails to account for the critical question of who possesses the power to actually make things happen. Could it be man's inflated ego deceiving him into thinking that he has the power to make anything happen in the first place (John 15:5, 19:11)? The problem lies with our understanding of who God is and what His promises are.

Therefore rethinking God's position in relation to man's place may be in order. This necessary refocusing of the distorted lens of hierarchy will influence the believer's attitude.

ONE'S ATTITUDE TOWARD GOD

A basic flaw too often overlooked manages to overshadow well-meaning believers. The requestor's attitude affects how he thinks about faith and how he understands God's answers to his prayers. God must be allowed to be God; by this is meant, He must be allowed to answer if He wants to answer, when He wants to answer, how He wants to answer, where He wants to answer, and why He wants to answer. Our requests are just that, requests. They must stay in the realm of requests and never become directives; otherwise, the equation will be thrown out of order and will not work. God is not to be dictated to. He is the Sovereign, not us.

Notice here, that one's faith and the results to prayer may be mutually exclusive. This is not to say that faith is unimportant in prayer; on the contrary, it is absolutely essential. When encouraging his readers to pray for wisdom, James the apostle admonished the requestor to do so in faith,

> For let not that man [who does not pray in faith] expect that he will receive anything from the Lord.
>
> —James1:7

However, this does not obligate God to answer, especially in the affirmative; He may still delay His answer or answer in the negative. This should not diminish our faith, we should rather adjust. Keeping in mind that the God of love, mercy, grace, and forgiveness has our best interest at heart; we should trust His judgment that He has a better plan for us.

Jesus assured His listeners that the heavenly father is pure in His dealings with us. He asked,

> "What man is there among you, when his son shall ask him for a loaf, will give him a stone? Or if he shall ask for a fish, he will not give him a snake, will he?" Jesus then affirmed, "If you then, being evil, know how to give good gifts to your children, how much more shall your Father who is in heaven give what is good to those who ask Him!"
>
> —Matthew 7:9-11

We cannot out-love God. The guiltless sacrifice of Christ as a substitute for guilty sinners has settled that question once for all. Since life is so precious, the ultimate demonstration of love is found in being willing to die to save someone else.

Jesus, the Son of God, submitted to this arrangement (Philippians 2:5-11). His attitude was in line with His Father's. When He faced the greatest challenge of His earthly life—the prospect of a shameful public death on a wooden cross to bear the sins of the world—He retreated to a familiar location where He and His disciples often met for prayer. The content of His prayer is common knowledge. His Father's apparent silence and Jesus' acceptance of the negative answer is also common knowledge.

> "My Father," He agonized, "If it is possible, let this cup pass from Me; yet, not as I will, but as You will."
>
> —Matthew 26:39

Even the Son of God did not dictate to God; rather, He subordinated His will to the will of His Father. Essentially, His Father denied Him His request.

Did His faith fail? Not at all! No one ever questioned the strength of His belief in God's ability to deliver. No protesting finger was pointed to dispute the scale of His faith. He had a request. He took His request to His Father and left the outcome up to His Father. Our requests must follow this same model. A better paradigm we cannot find. We may desire things and request them but God will only give us those things He deems good for us, at the time He thinks we ought to have them, if indeed He wants us to have them.

God is choreographing all the complexities of His universe. As much as things may appear chaotic, He has a plan for how things are to turn out. Our requests may or may not fit into His intricate plan. Or, they may very well be part of His plans for us but not necessarily at the time we expect. We must, therefore, be patient and trust His judgment.

SPIRITUAL PRIDE—A BARRIER

Not altogether different are those who exercise faith with the underlying thought that they are a favorite child of God and as a result deserve answers to their requests. Their attitude clouds their judgment about their rightful place in God's family. The elder brother in the story of the Prodigal Son narrated in Luke 15, never seemed to appreciate this principle. While his younger brother went away and squandered his portion of the family fortune, he stayed at home and served his father, toiling long and hard. Upon his brother's return, he received his father's loving welcome, was forgiven of all wrong doing and was afforded the choicest of the family favorites. The stay-at-home elder brother, on the other hand, resented the celebrations and reception his younger sibling enjoyed and whined to his father accusing him of misapplying his graces. His gripe to his father was that he had been loyal all along and never violated any of his laws, but as soon as his vagabond brother returned, he is treated to the best in the estate. His father's response was meant to correct the firstborn's attitude. He said,

> My child, you have always been with me, and all that is mine is yours. But we had to be merry and rejoice, for this brother of yours was dead and has begun to live, and was lost and has been found.
>
> —Luke 15:31-32

We must guard against the favorite child syndrome. All who belong to God are His only by His grace and not by their charm or spiritual savvy. This type of subtle pride gets under the skin of dedicated and well-meaning believers. But God does not operate like some humans do. He loves all His children equally.

I am privileged to be part of a large family; and, from time to time, as kids we were curious to know which one of us was Mom's favorite. We all secretly eyed Joseph's coat of many colors. But attempts to determine the answer to that question was customarily met with the same response. Always careful to look into our eyes as if she could see the deepest parts of our souls, Mom would provide that reassurance she instinctively knew we had been seeking. "I love you all equally the same," she would say, "I have no favorite, you are all different but I love you all the same." We must guard against this subtle pride which can cloud our view of reality. We do not want God to resist us; for it is written,

God resists the proud but gives grace to the humble.
—James 4:6; 1 Peter 5:5

Our attitude may well be a factor in how God chooses to answer our requests. We may have strong faith but equally possess strong narcissistic pride.

GOD—A LAW UNTO HIMSELF

The biblical book of Job is particularly instructive on this elusive spiritual principle. The opening lines of Job are painfully careful to point out that he was a righteous man— God does not say that about too many people.

That narrative shows how Job lived such a reverential life that he even made preparations to atone for his children's sins committed unawares. It was clear that he held enormous faith in God.

Job's life pleased God so much that the Almighty boasted to Lucifer about the human's loyalty to Him. True to his nature, the prince of darkness seized the opportunity to request a bout with the innocent man in order to seduce him to abandon his loyalty to God. To everyone's surprise, the Holy One granted Satan's infamous request and allowed him to inflict great pain upon the spiritual giant; for, God knew that Job's faith would hold firm. The devil went to work on the unsuspecting righteous man with a barrage of afflictions in attempts to topple the tower of his faith. In that nightmare of a chess game between God and the devil, Job lost his possessions, his children, and he was plagued with boils from the crown of his head to the soles of his feet.

When news of Job's misfortune hit the airwaves, three of his closest friends arrived at his premises; supposedly, to comfort him. But their words proved to be a minefield of blame and condemnation instead of the sympathy and support expected of close friends. They couldn't understand how Job could be innocent of offending God in some way. None of Job's attempts at explaining that he searched his heart and examined himself to see if he did something to incur the judgment of God satisfied them. They insisted that he MUST have been culpable. But he maintained his innocence and vowed that despite what was happening he would always trust God. This is what Job said of God,

Though He slays me, yet will I trust Him.

—Job 13:15

Now if there was ever anyone who could say he had reasons for questioning his continued loyalty to God, Job might be the likeliest candidate. Although he was deeply hurt and could have felt that God turned on him, his faith did not fail.

Many believers have quietly grappled with questions of fairness when it comes to what seems like God's meddling interference in Job's life. Out of reverence, they remain careful to avoid pointing a finger at God but remain at a loss to reconcile His unusual actions in the life of an innocent man with His own stellar character. Whatever else may be said about this true narrative, one thing is evident; a careful reading offers insight into God's sovereign right to be God. There is only one Supreme Being anywhere and He does as He pleases. One may say that the central message of Job is that God has a sovereign right to do as He pleases in the lives of people from time to time. It is the sentiment clearly expressed in the book of Daniel but demonstrated in Job.

The Most High God rules in the affairs of men.
—Daniel 4:17, 25

It was God who pointed out Job's flawless character to Lucifer as if making a cosmic dare with a man's life. God is a law unto Himself. He can do this. And no one can stop Him. Job's story is not God's usual modus operandi; it is a unique and isolated incident in Scripture. But it underscores the hard-to-swallow principle that God is the supreme ruler over all. A concept we in democratic countries find difficult to embrace even when it applies to GOD.

When faith doesn't seem to work we ought not to be hasty to lay blame to the amount of faith we possess. Rather we should remember that God may very well be delaying the item we requested for His own purposes.

We must keep in mind that God's central attribute constitutes His Holy character. From this, all His other attributes flow. God will not approve a request which is unholy and which is contrary to His character. Sometimes the thing requested is not good for us. As a loving father He cannot approve evil and will not grant requests which we will use only to gratify our selfish desires. James 4:3 helps us to understand this,

> You ask and do not receive, because you ask with wrong motives, so that you may spend it on your pleasures.

GOD HAS OUR BEST INTEREST AT HEART

But because He is sovereign and holy doesn't mean He is peering through the clouds with roving eyes to stamp out any sight of fun and leisure. God is not seeking opportunity to replace all smiles with frowns and light and bubbly hearts with somber hearts. He is the one who created us. And by nature He is compassionate, slow to anger, and abounds in loyal love (Exodus 34:5-7).

Because of this, the implications are wonderful. For, as the painting is a reflection of the mind and feelings of the artist; so is the creature a reflection of the mind and sentiments of the Creator. The Greeks sought to capture this with their concept of "logos" or word. A spoken word is first conceived in the mind of the speaker before it is given expression; so too is the sculpture in the mind of the sculptor before it was given expression. It is God who encoded our

DNA with the capacity to enjoy the things we enjoy. He, more than anyone, wants us to enjoy an abundant life.

He wants us, however, to enjoy them to their fullest, only in the legitimacy of their proper setting. This important principle reminds me of words I read somewhere. The idea is that sex is like fire. In the fireplace, fire is beautiful to look at, makes the room cozy and inviting, and is controlled and confined in a safe place. Outside the fireplace however, fire can ravish our lives with devastating effect, destroying in seconds things we worked hard for, things that may be precious to us. Sex outside the legitimacy of marriage destroys lives. So, God wants us to enjoy His gifts to us in their appropriate setting.

Many of us can recall times in our youth when we were convinced that our parents or, whoever was responsible for us, had too many rules for us to keep. During those moments we found it genuinely difficult to believe that they really loved us. We may have constructed what we thought were air-tight arguments debating that all the other kids were doing it (whatever 'it' was). In such arguments we, no doubt, proved that 'it' was harmless, that we were old enough, that we had proven to be reliable and responsible children, and basically provided all the reasons we should be allowed to do 'it' or go 'there.' But after all that, our parents still denied us our requests. "Surely," we thought to ourselves, "We are not loved; the rules are too rigid."

Then we grew up and gained a great amount of knowledge and understanding along the way. Now our perspectives have changed. Instead of thinking that our loved ones hated us; we are grateful that they cared enough to lovingly protect us even when we sincerely thought we knew better.

God is not the cosmic bully waving His big stick around to intimidate and keep us in line. He wants the best for us.

FASTING, SPIRITUAL OPPOSITION & FORGIVENESS

As a compassionate, gracious, Father, God treats all His children's requests with loving concern. But not all requests are created equal. To be sure, all require faith. Some things are easier to believe than others. But others, for one reason or another, are harder to hang our faith upon.

For those, it may require the removal of obstacles getting in the way of our faith. For, God does not grant any believer answers to their prayers without faith. So if we lack faith we must ask Him for it. We must seek it even if it takes self-denial in fasting and focused prayer. He grants insights and breakthroughs to those who put Him first. There must be a measure of sacrifice on our part. We must want it bad enough to set aside time to pray and fast. It is a call for a deeper consecration, one that builds our faith.

This Kind Does Not Go Out

Many are familiar with the narrative of a father who brought his child to Jesus' disciples because an evil spirit had been tormenting him; but their attempts at removing the demonic spirit resulted in failure. The child was then brought to Jesus who was successful in making the foul spirit vacate the boy. Before Jesus took authority over the demon and cast it out, He said to His disciples:

You unbelieving generation, how much longer must I be
with you? How much longer must I put up with you?
—Mark 9:19

Interestingly Jesus pointed to their unbelief, not their small
faith, but their lack of faith. Later He went on to explain,

This kind does not go out except by prayer and fasting.
—Mark 9:29

This situation required faith which they lacked. There were
forces blocking their understanding and affecting their faith.
They didn't see what God saw. Here was a boy who was at
the mercy of an EVIL spirit. They didn't understand that the
demons were subject to them. They needed to feel the way
God felt about the situation. They needed to desire to have
God's heart and mind about the condition of this child for
themselves. God wanted them to feel what He feels for the
state of this child who was invaded by an evil being.

For us to feel the way God feels about a given situation,
we must remove ourselves from those things which clutter
and distract us unawares. Taking off the television (or
computer), staying away from food, meditating on the
Scriptures, and praying constantly and specifically about
certain matters.

The spiritual discipline of fasting and prayer gives us that
focus and takes us beyond the ordinary. The disciples lacked
faith. It was probably in the presence of the crowd that Jesus
called the child's father to faith when He said to him,

All things are possible for the one who believes.
—Mark 9:23

The disciples' faith was non-existent. They needed undistracted time with God. They had to have faith to be able to cast out the demon. Likewise, when we don't receive answers to some prayers, God may be waiting for us to demonstrate persistence and show how much we desire it, how much we really believe Him. He wants undivided time with us.

Spiritual Forces Block Answers

There are other times when some prayers are not easily answered. These have to do with the activity of spiritual forces blocking the transaction. Such was the case with the prophet Daniel when he prayed and fasted concerning the plight of his people. Daniel understood this and was found fasting and supplicating the throne of God. An angel appeared to him twenty-one days into his fast and announced,

> Don't be afraid, Daniel, for from the very first day you applied your mind to understand and to humble yourself before your God, your words were heard. I have come in response to your words. However, *the prince of the kingdom of Persia was opposing me for twenty-one days.* But Michael, one of the leading princes, came to help me, because I was left there with the kings of Persia. Now I have come to help you understand what will happen to your people in the latter days.
>
> —Daniel 10:12-14

That phrase highlighted in the Daniel quote above describes spiritual opposition from the kingdom of darkness. The opposition actually held up Daniel's prayers from being carried out for the twenty-one days he prayed until there was a spiritual breakthrough.

Failure To Forgive

A more common occurrence may have to do with how we treat our neighbors. Numerous times in Scripture believers are told to forgive their fellow man. When, for instance, the disciples asked Jesus to teach them to pray, one of the things Jesus taught them to pray was,

> Forgive us our trespasses as we forgive those who trespass against us.
>
> —Matthew 6:12

Another time Jesus was passing by a fig tree He had previously cursed, Peter brought to His attention that the tree had withered. At this Jesus told them to have faith in God and then He added this,

> Truly I say to you, whoever says to this mountain, "Be taken up and cast into the sea," and does not doubt in his heart, but believes that what he says is going to happen, it shall be granted him. Therefore, I say to you, all things for which you pray and ask, believe that you have received them, and they shall be granted you. *"And whenever you stand praying, forgive, if you have anything against anyone; so that your Father also who is in heaven may forgive you your transgressions. "But if you do not forgive, neither will your father who is in heaven forgive your transgressions."*
>
> —Mark 11:22-26

Our failure to forgive others is a clear hindrance to prayer. We must be pure in our hearts and know that God is benevolent in His dealings with us. As David (the man after God's own heart) has taught us,

> If I regard iniquity in my heart; the Lord will not hear me.
> —Psalm 66:18

Jesus paid an enormous price to be able to forgive us of all our sins and remove our guilt. He won't forgive us if we refuse to forgive those who wronged us; especially since they did so at a much lesser cost to us than it cost God for our forgiveness.

SIN SEPARATES

There is another reason our faith may not seem to work, and that is when there is sin in our lives. Simply put, anything contrary to the nature and character of God constitutes sin. This, especially known sin, can obstruct the hand of blessing in a believer's life. Here again, the believer may exercise faith. His faith may not be in question. But because of the deceptive nature of sin, his loyalties are somewhat divided. When this happens there is a broken relationship between the believer and God.

> Your iniquities have made a separation between you and your God. And your sins have hidden His face from you so that He does not hear.
> —Isaiah 59:2

At this point, God is more interested in mending the relationship than granting requests that may be skewed to begin with.

This tendency of God finds a counterpart within human relationships. The specialness of the parent-child bond easily amplifies this unfortunate reality occurring everyday throughout the world. When a son or daughter violates the family code, a barrier, not previously there, appears and blocks the freedom of relating. There is a breakdown in communication forced upon them by the imposter of distrust. And before they can continue as they did previously, they must repair the damage caused by the violation. Sometimes the erring one never acknowledges his error nor does he apologize for his wrong. In these cases the relationship may continue but there will be little real growth. Therefore the wise parent does not ignore the infringement; but, lovingly seeks to address it and forgive it so they can continue to build a healthy and meaningful home.

God pursues a similar path. He does not endorse sweeping the disciple's fumbles under the proverbial rug; His preferred approach is more direct. Like the loving parent, He wants to remove the threat from the relationship. He wants us to confess our sins and continue to build from there.

> He who covers his sins shall not prosper, but whoso confesses and forsakes shall have mercy.
> —Proverbs 28:13

When faith doesn't seem to work we should remember that the Supreme One (who is the object of our faith) has the ultimate say in our lives. We do well to make sure our attitudes are in line with what He approves. Failure to forgive our fellowman constitutes a sure obstacle to answered prayers. There are times when our hearts are right but spiritual forces oppose us hindering our prayers. At those times, although God is able to remove the spiritual opposition, He calls us to pray and fast. These all conspire to contribute to the common culprits of failed faith. They demonstrate that our faith is not fully in Him but misplaced upon another object—ourselves. We must rely totally upon God.

I close with the words of the apostle Paul, who said:

> Your faith should not rest in the wisdom of men; but in the power of God.
>
> —1 Corinthians 2:5

Informed faith is not content to settle on untested ground; it fastens itself to the proven bedrock of an infallible God.

❧

CHAPTER 12 DISCUSSION QUESTIONS

1. Does the fact that God holds the power to grant or deny requests figure in whether our faith has failed?

2. How does the knowledge that God has our best interest at heart clarify whether our faith is working?

3. Where do sin, spiritual pride, unforgiveness and attitude figure in the equation of successful faith?

4. What role does prayer and fasting play in seeing answers to prayer and successful faith?

CONCLUSION

What a journey! The fabric of faith is strong. It is majestic. Its scope is immeasurable, its power indestructible, its reach accessible to all. Because it originates from the God of love, the journey of faith is adventurous.

I stated in the preface that a stranger on the streets of New York City challenged me with hard questions about my faith. Although those questions made me uncomfortable, I was glad for the challenge. I'd like to do the same with you; not make you uneasy, but I'd like to ask if your faith is an informed one? Have you proven it? Is it secured upon an indestructible foundation? Everyone believes in someone, some system, or something. If, God forbid, you were to die today and must face God, your maker, are you absolutely sure you would enter His glorious presence? Or, will you be eternally separated from the Son of God who loves you and gave Himself for you?

Placing all our faith in the death and resurrection of Jesus Christ as God directs us to do, ushers in that spiritual birth which originates in God. From that point on an exciting adventure of faith with the Almighty begins. This rich and meaningful life can only start after we ask God to forgive us our sins and we receive His gift of eternal life.

I lovingly and respectfully urge you to place your faith in Him now.

☙

REFERENCES

Cocoris, G. M. (1984). *Evangelism, A Biblical Approach.* Chicago, IL: Moody Press.

Josephus, *Antiquities of the Jews* 19.8.2, 343-361.

Lewis, C. S. (1960). *Mere Christianity.* New York, NY: The MacMillan Company.

McDowell, J. (1977). *More Than A Carpenter.* Wheaton, IL: Tyndale House Publishers, Inc.

Miles, C. A. (1912). *In The Garden.* Retrieved December 02, 2014, fromhttp://www.cyberhymnal.org

Oatman J. Jr., (1894). *Holy, Holy Is What The Angels Say.* Retrieved December 26, 2014 from http://nethymnal.org/htm/h/o/holholis.htm

Richie, L. & Ross, D. *Endless Love.* Retrieved December 04, 2014, from http://www.asklyrics.com

Sproul, R. C. (1980). *Explaining Inerrancy.* Oakland: International Council on Biblical Inerrancy.

Stoner, P. W. (1969). *Science Speaks: Scientific Proof of the Accuracy of Prophecy and the Bible.* Chicago, IL: Moody Press.

48420677R00130

Made in the USA
Middletown, DE
19 September 2017